LIFTING THE MIND FOG

ROBERT VINCENT SIMS

GARDEN REBEL ™ BOOKS

DEDICATION

*To my father, my shinning candle
in the dark.*

INTRODUCTION

JERRY BAKER

The inside edge, an even break, a look into the future, if I had have known then what I know now are all wishes and wants that every one of us have thought or spoken as we traveled along the path of maturity. For some this journey began very young, others it began at what is referred to as the mid-life crisis, or the day we woke up to the fact that our only true destiny is that someday we must die. The old saying that, "Everyone wants to go to heaven but no one wants to die to get there," are the truest words of wisdom I have ever heard or witnessed. No one wants to turn the key!

Robert Vincent Sims has for the last twenty some years been a delight, inspiration and pride and joy to know and mentor to, in his gardening, writing and broadcast career, but even more to the wisdom and insight that he displayed so young in his life and career.

In *Lifting the Mind Fog*, Vincent brings the six most important areas of life's table of contents, to help any one of any age or sex to achieve both the mind and heart set you will need to prepare yourself or re-instate yourself to begin and continue your journey course, the rest of life's path, in a healthy, happy,

1

prosperous, and fulfilling life.

The sincere and humorous style lets you relax, understand and enjoy the most important bits and bites you have ever read.

- Jerry Baker

AUTHOR: *JERRY BAKER'S GROWTH PLAN FOR PEOPLE*

ACKNOWLEDGMENTS

To my wife, Nalini, you're more than the sparkling diamond in my life you're the whole treasure chest!

To Jerry Baker, my mentor and best friend, you're far more than America's Master Gardener, you're the king. You've inspired me enough for ten lifetimes!

To Pat Fisher, your light has been my lighthouse beacon for growth. You have helped me more than you'll ever know in so many areas of my life, not the least of which has been the fine tuning of this book. I know an angel when I see one.

To Dr. Margaret Maney who affectionately calls me an extra-terrestrial and has always understood me from the first day twenty years ago as a student in her writing class. Mags, thanks for the "A" and for all the help with this book.

To Paul and Cher Duckworth, for being my sounding boards when I decide to pontificate on the ways of the world! You guys make me laugh and that makes you both very special.

To Jennifer Russell, my manuscript typist and secretary, thank you for your patience when I'm in the mind fog!

To Dr. Tony Previte, my good friend and original tennis partner, when the universe created you I'm sure there was a tag: unlimited, creative, exceptional human being!

To all of my friends whose actions inspired me to write a story that might help someone.

To all of my friends who contributed their methods of lifting the mind fog to chapter six. Each of you is special in my life, your success and passions show in the sparkle of your eyes. You're all superstars to me by walking the walk.

To my mother in heaven, you're the greatest!

To my father in Eustis, for not dropping the candle.

To our Father in Heaven, for all of the above, all there is, and all that ever will be.

Robert Vincent Sims

CONTENTS

1

THE MAGIC OF APPRECIATION

"THAT WHICH IS LOVED IS ALWAYS BEAUTIFUL."
- NORWEGIAN PROVERB

A few years back I got a telephone call from my mother who asked me to sit down because she had some news to tell me. Immediately my instincts picked up on her tone of voice, and my chest filled with heat, which within seconds permeated my entire being. "Yes Mom," I whispered with my voice cracking. "Sweetheart, I went to the doctor today and got some sad news. I have a rare form of cancer, and Dr. Vasquez wants me to check into the Mayo Clinic in Minnesota, immediately!" The next morning my wife Nalini and I met my folks in Fort Lauderdale and boarded the plane to Minnesota which was the longest and saddest flight any of us had ever taken. Mom had the five-hour operation, and I spent the five hours in the cathedral and in the hospital library. Within minutes of my research

I learned that bile duct cancer is a form of pancreatic cancer and very little research and information are available on this type. Furthermore, even with an operation, patients only survive about one and a half years or so. This same moment the realization hit me: this was the beginning of the biggest storm I've ever had to go through. My instinct was to help my mom in all conceivable ways, from helping her in and out of the wheelchair to giving her two to three pep talks a day. The cancer obstacle made it difficult for me to be optimistic, but I was determined to get the most out of every day, every hour, every minute. Time suddenly became very precious to our whole family. We were each other's support and most of the time mom was our support, given her natural optimistic outlook. We had been home a week from Minnesota and after the fatigue had tapered a bit, I decided that I needed to talk to somebody. This family crisis was lonely. My most compassionate and optimistic friend was Jon Alexander. Jon was the popular producer of the "Philips File," with Jim Philips, heard on central Florida radio. He was also an on air personality who had a tremendous following of his own. Together they were an invincible team. I had to record some radio commercials, so I called him up at the radio station to tell him I had a personal problem that I needed to just talk out with him. He said, "Sure Vince, I'll stay after work and

8

help you with the commercials then we'll go for chicken wings, and whatever the problem is, we'll figure it out!" At the restaurant I told Jon the whole story. True to his innate optimistic spirit, he suggested that the four of us, including my wife and his girlfriend Lou, needed to be a bridge to my mom. Although mom was five hours away by car, Jon suggested that we begin building her bridge. "Let's visit her at least every other weekend! We can bring her fruits and homemade foods, but the most important thing, Vince, is that she does not become an island. Let's make it our mission to keep her spirits up! Among the four of us we'll keep her laughing so hard she won't have time to be sick!" Right then we made plans for our first pilgrimage to see mom in two weeks. Wow! I was excited to have the support of a good friend. Jon's sincerity gave me a lot of strength and mom was thrilled with the news of our coming to see her.

So, we all went about our business and a week later I had a call from Jon.

"Vince, are you coming in to do commercials tonight?"

"You bet, Jon! I'll be there."

"Vince, let's go to the chicken wing place. I need to talk to you."

"Jon, I'll see you at 7:00 p.m.."
The server sat us at the same table where I had told Jon the news about my family situation. Within minutes, Jon proceeded to

drop the bombshell.

"Vince, I haven't told anyone this yet but three days ago, I was diagnosed with terminal esophagus cancer. The doctor tells me I just have a few months."

Suddenly, I needed to be Jon's support system. Even though Jon's cancer weakened him physically, he had his good days and bad days and he kept his promise to raise mom's spirits.

They corresponded by phone and gave each other strength when the other one needed it. On their first conversation mom asked, "Jon, what are you going to do?" Jon promptly replied, "Well, mom I'll tell you. I need new tires for my car, but I'm not going to buy them!" They had a great belly laugh over that, and on every future conversation, my mom told Jon, "Go out and buy those tires!"

Over the next few months, Jon and I had many conversations and many of the things we'd talked about had a tremendous impact on me. As we were closing the conversation for one evening, Jon mentioned something in particular that I'll never forget.

"Vince, I hope the world can realize that we need to be thankful for what we all have and not what we want."

Jon was referring to the chase for riches and power that seems to be so prevalent in our society. Jon and mom became great telephone buddies and the inspiration that derived from observing their progressive growth as human beings is beyond explanation.

My best friend, Jon, and my mom died within a few weeks of each other, but their inspiration, humor, persistence, and acceptance have had a profound effect on my life. Both lived their life as a great adventure, and they appreciated all that life had to offer before their diagnoses as well as after.

APPRECIATING THE LITTLE THINGS

When I was a landscape teacher in night school, I used to do an exercise that would always get a lot of attention and stir up a lot of laughter. "Class, tonight we are going to look at the bottoms of a bunch of leaves and by the end of this evening you will appreciate the bottoms as much as the tops!" Well, after they all picked themselves off the floor from laughing so hard, the lesson began. I brought in all types of foliage. We saw the spores on the bottom of the fronds of the highly divided ferns. We saw the spore pattern aligned intricately and perfectly. We looked at long, variegated foliage with a perfect white streak down the middle. Under the microscope a whole new world was opened as we observed the incredible highly ribbed, raised veins on the bottom leaf of an anthurium. We marveled at the texture and various color blends and shapes of the croton. We even looked under the microscope at a weed's flower that was nothing less than a perfect yellow daisy. The only difference was that it was several thousand times smaller. I did this exercise because I wanted to make a point that beauty can be observed from many angles. The students were flabbergasted at the depth of beauty that they had missed in all their casual observations.

Sometimes we become jaded by the beauty even as it surrounds us. It's important to be aware that beauty can be seen at various depths, from many angles. Once we learn to appreciate it in whatever form it is, a whole new exciting world is open to us. We all need to turn the leaves over because there is a lot of beauty to be appreciated underneath, and the great thing is that it has always been there and always will be there, all the time. The sounds of a baby's laughter is music of joy. Soft background music with the candle flame flickering on the dinner table, the colors of a Macaw, the fiddlehead of a fern as it unravels, and even the squeal of our dogs as we return home from our jobs bring beauty and joy to us.

One of the little happenings that occurred years ago still makes me smile when I think about it. As I pulled into their circular driveway to visit my in-laws to help landscape their house, I noticed that my father-in-law, was backing out of the backyard driveway. Their golden retriever, Sparky, sat in the backseat. "Hey, where are you going? We have all these plants to unload," I shouted. As he waved, while backing out, he calmly said, "I'll be back in a few minutes, I'm taking Sparky for his afternoon neighborhood ride." About ten minutes later he and Sparky pulled into the driveway. Once again, I asked him, "Where did you go?" I always thought that if you had a dog in the car you must be going to the veterinarian. Once again, he told me he took Sparky for his ride. I asked, "You mean to tell me you drove the dog around just for the hell of it?" "No," he exclaimed, "I do it because he enjoys it!" In its humor, this was a beautiful moment.

Years ago Dolly Parton and Willie Nelson sang a song, "Everything's Beautiful In Its Own Way." Dolly and Willie, I couldn't agree with you more.

TAKING TIME FOR OURSELVES

Like any flower, we can't continue to bloom and prosper without the proper diet. We need to take the time to renew, invigorate and develop a love for ourselves. By becoming aware and truly appreciating all the beauty that surrounds us, we'll receive the greatest gift of all, which is a knowing or inner peace so strong that other peoples' opinions, sarcasms, outbursts, and overall general actions are easily repelled. Likewise, another's love and serenity can be easily absorbed for personal growth. Some people find strolling out into the garden early in the morning particularly calming to the senses. A garden of shrubs, trees, and flowers has an unlimited amount of beauty to appreciate. First of all, there's that special morning light. The dew on the foliage even has a different appearance, depending on the type of leaf it engulfs. There are the various sounds of the birds as they flutter from branch to branch, then to the foliage, and then to the ground. There are the sounds of a slow trickling waterfall that also adds movement to a garden. Even the dark brown or golden mulch bark that is no longer living serves a purpose of color, texture, and moisture retention. In fact, it is living, by being a part of the artwork that grows. The young buds of a magnolia or the pure white of a gardenia both excite the emotions. The fragrance is often so striking that the aroma goes beyond the physical boundaries of our home and out into the neighborhood! Those tiny fragrance cells and the various color pigments in little flowers just may be one of the most powerful emotion pleasers that nature has.

Music is another very passionate part of many peoples' lives. We all have a favorite song or perhaps several that have special meaning to our lives. By closing our eyes and not concentrating but instead absorbing the individual tones and beauty of the collective sound enriches the soul. Loving and appreciating the melodic poetry of another person's words, usually someone we don't know and may never meet, gives us an incredible knowing or connection or link that soothes our inner core. Music is a reminder that people, regardless of their culture, age, physical size or beauty, all have undulating wave-cycles in their life that symbolize the same emotions of love and fear. One of the great, ongoing lessons I've been able to observe in my life has been from my mother-in-law, Jean Persaud. She grew up in Guyana, South America and was raised with the concept that you can't give away what you don't have. From the time she was a small child she has done things for herself in the form of diet and exercise and personal growth. In return she is calm, peaceful, fun, nonmaterialistic, positive, and loving. She and her husband raised five fantastic kids, all about eleven months apart I might add, and all are considered dynamos in their families and communities. Even when her babies were small and all competing for their fair share of love and glory, she at the beginning and end of her demanding days still found some quiet time to devote to herself. Even if it was only an hour, she still consistently took the time to pamper herself. Her days were action-packed. She spent her hours teaching, playing, singing, reading, and entertaining the babies. There were plenty of nights when her husband was away at the university when she experienced the drama of all the kids crying at once. I once asked her what she did when that happened and she replied, "I sometimes was so overwhelmed I got in the middle of the bed and cried with them." She never gave up. Her goal and mission were to give the kids as much love as possible, then give some more. A mother's devotion is a beautiful gift to appreciate. Her caring has paid off in great dividends. All five kids are uniquely progressive and have the common denominator of wanting to care for and help others. As children they saw that their mother had a nutritious diet and exercise regimen that was an inherent part of her lifestyle. After playing with the kids, she exercised in their playroom and they all joined in the daily routine. As difficult as this concept of juggling our own life while still being totally devoted to family may be, I know it can be done. Jean Persaud is a living example.

APPRECIATING ANIMALS

For me, growing up in the country was the perfect background for raising a variety of animals. My father was raised on a 160-acre farm in Michigan, and grew up with the love and excitement of animals. His appreciation for them has rubbed off on me and my family.

As a kid, I raised exotic chickens from all over the world. I had rabbits, rabbits, and more rabbits. I always had two or three dogs. At least once a month my dad and I would go to the dog pound just to give a little attention to some of the homeless. Dad and I regularly visited farms and local botanical gardens that had a variety of animals including peacocks, which were my favorite. One day while out on one of our explorations we turned down a shady dirt road. Suddenly, we heard the most blood curdling scream. It sounded like a woman crying for help. The hairs stood up on the back of our necks and that's when we saw the peacock up on the oak branch. Wow! We were relieved that we didn't have to save a damsel in distress.

When I was about ten years old mom,

dad and I took a vacation to visit my Uncle Rod and Aunt Helen in Murphy, North Carolina. My dad and I got up early one Saturday morning and walked a couple of blocks to the local county flea market. I remember it like it was yesterday. The market was non-commercialized and had people just selling their own garage-stored stuff. There were fantastically grown fresh peaches, plums, and apples. Other isles had old antiques and plenty of old automobile parts. We walked to the center isle and that's when I saw him. He was a friendly mountaineer dog, a full blooded black Labrador retriever. I started playing with him and he started rolling on his back and hoping I would just pet him forever! The farmer said, "Dat der dog is for sale. He'd be a great dog fer ya, kid." "How much is he sir?" I innocently asked. "He's on special today, boy. You can have him fer ten bucks!" Well, I looked all around and couldn't find dad. I finally found him on the other isle buying a wrench. "Dad, dad come and see this dog! He loves me dad. He can't stop licking me. Dad, dad he's for sale and he's only ten dollars!" Dad looked down at me and asked, "Would you take good care of him if we get him?" " Oh, I'll do everything, I'll feed him and brush him. You bet, dad. He's my buddy!" My dad then said, "I'll tell you what. Why don't you go ask the farmer if he'll take five dollars for the dog and if he does you can have him."

I ran as fast as I could back to the farmer. In fact, I ran so fast that as I got up to the farmer's booth, I tripped and skidded hands first into the sand in front of the farmer's truck tailgate. The big black Lab immediately started licking my face, neck, and hair and I laughed and laughed as I hugged him. I timidly looked up at the farmer and whispered, "Excuse me sir. May I have the dog for five dollars?" The farmer gave me a long pause as he stroked his beard and said, "Yeah, I reckon so boy." Right then my dad walked up and asked, "Well, did you get yourself a dog." "I sure did dad," I squealed. We then unwrapped the dog's chain from the old truck bumper and headed back to my Aunt and Uncle's farmhouse. I ran up the front porch yelling, "Mom, mom. Look what I have!" My mother gave my dad an ice cold stare and asked, "You didn't?" Dad shook his head, yes. "But we already have two dogs," she whispered. "Lillian, I just left the kid for five minutes, and he comes walking up with this dog. What am I supposed to do?" "Take him back. I'm not traveling with a smelly dog in my car all the way back to Florida," she screamed. At that moment my dad turned to me and said, "Hey, what are you going to name him? Angus?" "Yeah, that's a good name, dad!" Angus, as if he had acting lessons from Lassie, then ran up to mom and frantically licked her hand. She bent down and told Angus, "You're cute, but you're smelly."

19

The rest of the afternoon I played ball with Angus and gave him a bath. The next morning we loaded our suitcases in the trunk of the Oldsmobile. I opened the back door to put down an old sheet on the seat and no sooner finished when Angus jumped in and sat quietly and patiently for mom and dad to finish saying their goodbyes. We pulled out of the driveway with Uncle Rod and Aunt Helen waving and my mom smiling and holding her nose. When the car was put in drive, Angus gave two short barks as if to say goodbye. We got down the road a little ways and Angus placed his head on my lap, as I stroked his head he fell asleep. He found his family.

2

UNCOVER THE PASSION AND ACQUIRE THE KNOWLEDGE

IF YOU ARE RELUCTANT TO ASK THE WAY, YOU WILL BE LOST.

- MALAYSIAN PROVERB

When I was a little kid, I had a reputation. Everywhere I would go, I would ask questions! Usually the topics had to do with nature and plants in particular. As time went on my interest in gardening developed into a passion and my questions became even more numerous. Mr. Estep, my mentor from the age of ten, often answered the bulk of my questions without ever complaining. Every day when I got out of school, I literally ran home to change my clothes, jump on my bike and head out to my afternoon excursions to "The Little

21

Nursery," which was the actual name of Mr. &
Mrs. Estep's backyard business. Mr. Estep
was in his seventies at the time and still put in
a full day's work. By late afternoon his rest
periods became longer, and he systematically
quizzed me and taught me the ropes of the
business. We were the best of buddies, and I
helped him unload the truck, stack the nursery
pots, and mix the fertilizer in the wheelbarrow.
In between working we would take breaks and
naturally I continued to ask questions about all
the plants, soil, fertilizer, bugs, and pro-
pagating methods. By dinner time Mr. Estep
was worn out by all of my questions and would
go take his shower and prepare for dinner.
During that half hour period Mrs. Estep took
over, and we sat on the back porch steps and
just talked. We talked about her cacti
collection, the beauty of the huge queen crape
myrtle they had in their landscape, the bugs on
the tomatoes, and just about anything else that
had to do with our passion. I know that I was
long winded, and still am to this day, but never
once did they shoo me off prematurely. On the
weekends my grandparents would come over
to my house for the family barbecue and I
would corner them and ask even more
questions as they also had a strong interest in
growing plants. Occasionally, my grandmother,
Rebecca Stevenson, would ask me if I was
asking Mr. Estep, my mentor, plenty of
questions. "You can't learn if you don't ask

questions," she firmly expressed. "Oh, yes grandma. Mr. Estep is my best buddy. He helps me a lot." Grandma would then always have a follow-up statement, "Make sure you never make a pest of yourself." Then I would say, "Oh no grandma I never do, I always leave when Mr. Estep calls Mrs. Estep in to come fix his dinner!"

PERSONAL PASSION

Each and every one of us has our own personal passions, all within. We just have to tap into them. Passions sometimes remain undiscovered even at an advanced age. Sometimes people will ignore their passions and replace them with excuses of why they can't follow their passions. "I have to make a living," "I wish I had more time," "Someday, when I retire I'm going to do that." Folks that someday needs to become today, right now!

MAKE UP YOUR OWN MIND

Anytime we are at crossroads and have yet to make a final decision on a particular path to take, many relatives, friends and neighbors will often interject their thoughts and feelings. This is terrific! There is only one little problem: their passions and ours may be going in opposite directions. They'll say well-meaning things like "Oh, that's not for you" or worse yet, "Why in the world would you want to do that?" Words can be so powerful but we individually give them the power we want to give them. Others' suggestions can certainly help us, but until we completely develop our inner passions, others' advice can sometimes hurt us. Once our passions are fully developed, they'll grow exponentially! The more we learn, the more excited we get! The confidence begins to build and that inner little light bulb that we all have will never flicker, regardless of any obstacle in our path.

EVERYBODY HAS A GREEN THUMB: YOURS JUST MAY NEED RIPENING

Over the years I have opened many a garden lecture with that statement. One day while addressing a crowd of five hundred, at a women's club luncheon, I walked up to the microphone, took a deep breath and slowly enunciated every syllable, "Everybody Has A Green Thumb, Yours Just May Need Ripening." After I said it, I took a long Paul Harvey pause, for added drama. To my bewilderment a tall grey-haired English lady with a magnificently deep voice raised her hand while standing up and proclaimed,

24

"Excuse me Mr. Rebel, but my thumb has been dormant for more than sixty plus years and I really don't think it's going to ripen anytime soon!" Wow! What an opening. She single handedly brought the house down with roaring belly laughter. After the audience got their composure, I asked her if I could be her straight man in a Las Vegas comedy show, and we kiddingly agreed to formulate the partnership after my talk. I then proceeded to remind her that her thumb has only been dormant for sixty (eh hum) plus years and that dormancy is not the same as deadwood! I explained that her thumb, "just needs water, food, light, and knowledge, along with a little persistence. It's very much alive. Your thumb has its whole life ahead of it to successfully grow!" At this point everyone was smiling and the room had the aura of a synchronistically flawless party. I asked the wonderful English lady if she would please stand up again and repeat after me. She promptly popped up out of her seat and followed my lead, **"MY THUMB'S NOT DORMANT. I HAVE NO DEADWOOD AND I WILL WIN YARD OF THE MONTH, THIS YEAR!"**

IT'S NEVER TOO LATE TO UNCOVER THE PASSION

My best friend and mentor is America's Master Gardener, Jerry Baker. He is the Public Broadcast System national TV gardener, national radio personality, World Book Encyclopedia garden writer, and was the phenomenal garden spokesperson for K-Mart for more than 25 years. I love to remind him that as a teeny, weeny child I used to watch him on Dinah's Place, Mike Douglas, and Johnny Carson's Tonight Show. Although gardening was always a passion, he as a young man had another passion, law enforcement, which became his full time career. He became a top notch detective and would go undercover as a gardener. He loved helping people and looked forward to going to work everyday but after being stabbed, shot in the head, pushed down an elevator shaft and left for dead, he soon decided to develop his other passion, gardening. In his early forties he was able to focus and develop another life interest every bit as fulfilling and every bit as successful. Jerry, of course became a best-selling author, TV / radio personality, and all around horticultural entertainer. I've always admired the fact that his inner little light bulb never flickers and his light of knowledge is

26

continually growing brighter all the time. This attitude is a trait of inspirational people and self motivating people who live every minute to its fullest potential. Remember, as our natural passion develops it grows at an incredible exponential rate. When focused in a positive direction, this energy, this inner light bulb can never burn out.

FOCUS, FOCUS, FOCUS

There is an ancient Armenian proverb "If you run after two rabbits you won't catch either one." Spreading ourselves too thinly has very little or no personal growth benefit. If important decisions in our life are put on the back burner, that's where they stay. In my business of landscape design I often talk about an epidemic of gargantuan proportions. I call it "Landscape Procrastination." So many folks talk about wanting an all organic vegetable garden, or a gazebo surrounded with red roses just like the ones in the garden magazines. People tell me all the time, "I wish I had planted my fruit trees when I first moved in. I would be eating fruit by now." Remember, we have to sow the seeds or plant the seedlings before we can get the fruit! Talking about doing it is only a dream or a fantasy until we physically take the time to plan and then ultimately we can prosper.

PASSION AND ENTHUSIASM ARE DIFFERENT

Passion about anything is a fulfillment that touches the very core of our being. It is a knowing, an excitement, a solid all feet on the ground stability. It is our natural state to be happy and fulfilled. Once we uncover our lives' purpose, whatever it may be, the lights start to go on, one at a time, and the events in our lives seem to always be progressive. A wholeness and undefeated attitude become the norm and not the exception. We wake up in the morning with a clean slate, no rain, no fog, no twisters going on in the inner sanctum of our minds. Oh, once in a while a mind storm develops. It shows itself in the form of worry, doubt, and loss of self confidence. At this point we need to know that we can ride out the storm as long as our "house" is built on a solid foundation.

Always be aware that our positive attitudes need to be consistent for prolonged periods of time. The longer our positive energies flow, the longer we'll be progressive in our daily lives. As a young boy, I learned from a series of wonderful family and neighborhood mentors that what we think about expands. If we consistently think negatively, that's what will manifest itself in our daily lives. When we deflect other peoples' judgements and eliminate our own customized personal judgements of other persons, places, and things, we experience great growth.

All of us have observed intense enthusiasm in people we meet in a social setting. Enthusiasm is important because it's a prerequisite to passion. Enthusiasm will always be our ally if it is sincere and from that inner core of our being that I mentioned earlier. False enthusiasm is just that, phoney. It won't help us, and it doesn't last.

WE ARE ALL ARTWORKS IN PROGRESS.

Focusing and guiding all of our positive energy into our sincere passion will always result in progressive growth. As our personal growth expands, we almost become the observer looking over the artwork in progress. That's what all of us are, "artworks in progress." We never need to desire to finish the "masterpiece," so to speak. A finished masterpiece implies that's all there can ever be. It's finished. Let's put a frame around it, and spend our time admiring it. Once we put limitations or a frame around our personal growth, our personal artworks are finished. I prefer to think of us as expanding live works in progress, always adding new colors, expanding our scopes and adding new dimensions on a progressive basis.

Making personal commitments to grow will create an awareness and knowledge that will become our solid foundation. We will give of ourselves and the more that we can sincerely offer to others, the more we'll receive.

What a shame that giving to others is regularly overlooked. Many people make it a practice to give to family, friends and even strangers around the holiday season. This once or twice a year generosity, helps prevent them from feeling guilty for a whole year. Is that what life has come to, we can now buy a whole guilt-free year?

We can give to our family, friends, and charities year round and it doesn't necessarily have to be in the form of money. Every person has an experience that enables them to help another person, in some way. Simply being a good listener, is a trait that can help many people. In addition, a card, a letter of encouragement, or the offer of a helping hand is always appreciated. Our bonus is that this giving will do wonders for lifting our own mind fog!

3

THE BLAME GAME

"HE WHO DIGS A HOLE FOR ANOTHER MAY FALL IN HIMSELF."

-RUSSIAN PROVERB

When we were little children, even before we could talk, we started blaming somebody or something when life just didn't go our way. One of the problems was that, we never seemed to remember "ourselves," blaming everything on something else. Oh, my friends, our lack of memory really is not a problem. That's why we have children. They remind us! Our little toddler Dcota loves to blame Rebel and Zeke, our Yorkshire terriers, when something goes wrong in his world. The other day while eating a scone, Dcota took a big bite then chose to give the remainder to Rebel. Rebel, not wanting to disappoint Dcota, gladly scurried up the stairs, jumped up on the bed, and proceeded to eat the scone on my pillow. Meanwhile, Dcota is screaming at the top of his lungs and pointing up the stairs and saying, "Rebel, Rebel, Rebel." Poor Rebel got all that blame for just doing what he does best, eating any extra food we accidentally drop or give him. He especially loves scones softened with baby's drool. It's like salsa to him! Then poor little Rebel almost got a double whammy. I saw him with crumbs all over my pillow and he was giving me a look like, "Why aren't you at work? Don't you have some plants to plant or something?" Well I got all hot inside, then thought, "Boy this looks familiar." Yes! Then that Harry Chapin song *The Cat's in The Cradle*, came to me in a flash. The realization was like a symphony going on in my head and my final verse was "My dog was just like me. Yeah, my dog was just like me . . . "

No, Rebel did not get any more blame. After all he has slept with us since he was a puppy. It's his bed too and after all he's watched his daddy, me, eat in bed for eight years! We are all our own examples, when it comes to realizing, organizing, and solving problems. It is a matter of being aware that we and only we are responsible for our own actions.

IT'S FUN TO BLAME

No, it's not Monopoly or Trivial Pursuit that is the most popular game. It's the blame game. It must be the most fun to play because so many of us within seconds of waking up start to play and often won't finish until we retire at night. First thing in the morning we ask our spouses why they kept the air conditioner set like a meat freezer. Oh, and how about that toothpaste, "You knew we were low. Why didn't you buy it?" When we get to work in the morning, the first thing we blame for making us late is the traffic, even though we left ten minutes later than usual. When we're busy at work, we can't take lunch. "That boss has been piling it on me this week!" Later in the day when we miss an important appointment, "My secretary didn't remind me this morning." So I have concluded that the blame game is definitely like Jeopardy and certainly the most popular game since so many of us are chronically addicted to it all the days of our lives.

Blaming others will never help us in the long run; it will only hold us back. Responding with our own abilities to solve a problem, creates the solution. It's efficient, it's what we want and it's the only way to be progressive. Recognizing our judgements will help to lift the fog a lot sooner.

FAVORITE CHARACTERS TO BLAME

Our Spouses:
*If they had done this like we asked, we
wouldn't be in this predicament now!
*If they made more money, we could have a
bigger house and a newer car!
*If they would mow, trim, feed, and seed
the grass, our yards wouldn't look like
the city dump!
*If they would stay off the golf course, we
would be able to spend more time
together!

Our Bosses:
*If they would spend less time with their
cronies and more time noticing our
hard work, we'd get a raise!
*If they would go out of town more often,
the pressure would be less and we
could get more done.
*If they weren't such a "suck-up" we could
have had their jobs!

Our Co-workers:
*If they would quit bothering us with that
trivial stuff, we could get our own work
done.
*If they weren't so clannish, we could move up

in this company.

*If they would work instead of spending time gossiping about their personal life, our department would run smoother.

Our Moms:

*If they weren't so selfish we could spend Thanksgiving at our house.

*If they would just change their clothes and hairstyles, they would look like they're part of this century.

*If they would quit nagging us, we would get better grades in school.

Our Dads:

*If they had gone to Little League with us more often, we would have been able to graduate from high school.

*If they had given us that loan we wouldn't have to work two jobs to buy that car.

*If they would stop harassing us about our boyfriends / girlfriends, we could concentrate on our jobs more.

Our Store Clerks:

*If they had a brain, they'd be dangerous.

*If they knew the prices, they wouldn't have to call for price checks.

*If they had a personality, they could get a
real job.

Our Teachers:
*If they weren't so boring, we could focus in
class.
*If they would talk slower, we could write it all
down.
*If they would not put essay questions on
the test, we could pass.

Little Old Ladies in the Buick Electras:
*If they would get off the road, we could get
there.
*If they would occasionally look in the mirror,
they would see that there is a mile of
traffic behind them.
*If they would voluntarily give up their licenses,
then there would be more space on the
road for important people.

Our Doctors:
*If they would find out what's wrong with
us, we could start feeling better.
*If they wouldn't book so many people at
one time, we wouldn't have to wait 45
minutes.
*If they had asked us the right questions, we

would have gotten to the root of the
problem.

Our Siblings:
*If they didn't marry money, they wouldn't
be so successful right now.
*If they had not pumped mom and dad dry,
financially, we could have been given
some money, too.
*If they weren't so ambitious, we wouldn't look
so bad!

Our Sisters-in-law:
*If they would quit nagging our brothers, they
would quit drinking.
*If they would lose weight they would look
better.
*If they would go back to school, they could get
a better job.

Our Sons:
*If they would quit spending so much money
on their girlfriends, they would be able
to save.
*If they would hurry and finish school, they
would get better jobs.
*If they would help out more at the house, it
wouldn't look like a pig pen.

Our Daughters:
*If they would settle down with Mr. Right, they
     would be happy.
*If they would call us more, we would be
     happier.
*If they would just listen to us, they could finally
     get somewhere in life.

Our Weather:
*If it wasn't so cold, we wouldn't be sick all the
     time.
*If it wasn't so hot, we could get out in that yard
     and make it look like humans live here.
*If the weather wasn't so gloomy, we could get
     something accomplished. (This reminds
     me of that lady that rear-ended my new
     truck while I was stopped at a traffic
     light. When asked what happened,
     she replied, "I think it's the weather. It's
     just so gloomy today)."

REDIRECT THE BLAME

Rather than spending our existence blaming others for everything that goes wrong in our lives, we need to try and redirect all that energy into positive thoughts. It has been said we are what we eat. Perhaps it's more accurate to say we are what we think! We can start right now this minute. There is no reason to start when we wake up tomorrow morning. For the next 24 hours, try to redirect all blaming thoughts into positive energy. For the rest of the 24-hour period, make a conscientious effort not to blame anything or anybody for anything regardless of how small or how serious the problem is. This simple little task is not so simple. By catching ourselves at our own game, judging and blaming, we become aware and will recognize the absurdity of always blaming others for every little thing that goes wrong. Every time we do, that little light will go on and remind us "We're back peddling again." Well, we may ask, "Who should we blame? Ourselves?" No, why blame anybody or anything. We already know it's non-productive. We already know we can't be progressive when our "thought space" is taken up with negativity. Consider the concept that every day the cards may not fall out exactly the way they do on our best days. Hey, the cards do fall differently every day and there are plenty of days with 2x4's, glass, nails, and other garbage in the road. We have two basic choices: We can go around the road blocks by dealing with them or moving them or we can aggressively ride right through them, pretending to ignore them. If we choose the latter, we will end up with plenty of scratches, dents, and flat tires. One of our main frustrations is that we schedule our day-to-day routines and appointments so tightly that when a road block does occur, we begin to catastrophize the remainder of the day rather than take a few minutes to think and figure out a reasonable solution so that we can be at peace. By planning for success with the thought process that "Whatever it is we can handle it," a positive and very powerful attitude will solidify within our entire being. My friend, Chris Miliotes, is a perfect example of this trait. Here is a man who is well known in the community as a doer. He works long hours in the restaurant business. He's involved in numerous organizations, he's loved his wife Elaine for thirty plus years, helped raise an incredible family, and is very active in his church. Besides all this he takes time for his personal passion. He raises orchids and receives incredible enjoyment by growing them, admiring them, and then giving them away! It is obvious to me that a good part of Chris's success is due to his dedicating, his time helping others. Regardless of the time of day, the day of the week, or the season, Chris is always in a good "aura." This "aura" of success is his inner light bulb. Everybody has an inner light bulb but some flicker brighter than others. Others burn out. What is this incredible difference where some people's light shines so brightly that other people are magnetized? Those lacking this light find the fog thickening. The answer is simple. It's all in the attitude. By not wasting time, blaming and pointing fingers, we'll be able to free ourselves up to peddle steady. Remember, we don't necessarily have to peddle faster; we have to peddle steady. It's this positive attitude that comes only from within, that will keep us consistently positive.

THE DEVIL MADE ME DO IT

Many people have simply conditioned themselves to blame others when everything doesn't go smoothly. Whenever we are figuratively pointing our finger at someone, we are not ridding ourselves of anger. We are simply increasing the heat of the fireball inside ourselves. Very often the people who are the recipients of our verbal anger are the ones that would always be a help to us in a desperate situation. We have all heard family members say, "You hurt our feelings. We're very unhappy with you!" Sometimes they say, "I

41

can't believe you did that to us." Of course the most absurd is, "Do you understand how you are making us feel?"

Everything that happens positively or negatively in our life is simply a result of our own perception. When anything comes across our life path, how we process it determines the smoothness or turmoil in our lives. Could it be that any of us could ever reach a state of awareness, calmness, and total non-absorption that we would never have a problem again? Well, no probably not, since none of us can walk on water. However, the way we process life's obstacles and how we deal with them can very much be mastered. Just like so many other things in life it comes down to practice, practice, practice. There have always been natural disasters, back stabbing friends and family, bosses that were tyrants, and day to day obstacles with people. Guess what? Even in the future all that "stuff" can all go away. That is, it can all go away in our perception. As our personal growth expands all that "stuff" will still be like woven thread throughout the world's stage, but there will be one major difference in our lives. We won't notice it! Or at least when it does pop up, pulling at our shoulder, we will instantly become aware of it and we will recognize the chaos for what it is, nonproductivity. This awareness is the "light bulb" that is within all of us. We'll know it when it comes. As it brightens, the fog will begin to lift and our entire thought process becomes more clear.

PEDDLE STEADY

A progressive life is like riding a bicycle. Fully functioning people are not peddling backwards and they're not peddling on a stationary bike. They are peddling steadily. The fact of the matter is that every single person that has ever been on the earth or will be on the earth in the future has or will have a series of problems. The fully functioning people or the progressive people, learn from every single happening in their life. There is a lesson to be learned and simply when we don't remember or process our lessons to help us, we just repeat the chaos. It's just like when Henny Youngman says, "Doctor, doctor, it hurts when I do this!" The doctor says, "Well don't do that!" So that's what it all comes down to. All the negativity that we play over and over, that mind-fog chaos that stays on our mind channel and plays the same scene, the same movie over and over, the one with the same star, us. When the light bulb comes on, we say to ourselves, "Wait a minute, I've played this exact same scene in this same movie before." The revelation or awareness is the catalyst that will get us to change the channel. When our mind tries to short circuit

43

and kick back to that same non-productive back peddling channel, we need to just flick it back to our core channel, the channel that has always been with us deep within the fog.

THE CORE CHANNEL

When something goes wrong in our lives, we need to quickly get back to our core channels. It really doesn't matter if we perceive the event that is happening to be big or small, once we center ourselves on our inner core. Yes. It's the inner workings of our "light bulb." We will begin to be able to solve the perceived problem. So many people live in total life chaos because of being relocated or fired from their job. What they perceived to be life impasses became positive turning points for their future. In a time of crisis it is not only time consuming but also non-productive to continually flick to different negative mind channels, or just as bad, keep it on the same negative channel. So who ya gonna call? "Channel Busters!" "Channel Busters" are located at the very core of our beings. By centering ourselves we are able to gain from the knowledge we've recently acquired and will be able to remain with our light bulb bright and will continue to peddle steady! When we function from our "center," we can best direct our daily movies. Hey, we are all the stars of our own movies so why not give ourselves top billing by also being the executive director and executive producer. We play these roles every day anyway in our lives' movies so we need to know now that it is us and only us that are the electricity to our own lamps. External forces or other people can only interfere or direct our personal movies if we allow it to happen. They love to write their own parts into our personal movies but they can't do it if we don't hire them. It is simply a matter of personal choices. It is a knowing that when we operate from our gut or our center, all happenings will align in our favor.

KEEP THE BALL IN MOTION

When I was a kid in college, I had the passion and the desire to play tennis every day. My buddy, Bob Becker, was my after school and evening tennis coach and I played and learned for the fun of it. One of the things Bob would always drill into me as I would chase the ball from line to line is "center yourself, center yourself, center yourself!" He always said that if I hit the ball from the sideline that when he returns it, I'll be in a better position to handle it from whatever angle it comes as long as I always remember to center myself on the court. He was right. It is the best angle to see when the ball comes from any one of several angles. The result: I was better off by being able to comfortably and accurately return the balls.

The same is true of life. When we are centered, we can better deflect anything that comes our way. By operating from our sidelines, we only create a larger problem. In fact, problems at this stage often become compounded and the daily dramas become addictive. We always need a bigger drama to top the last one. It's like they build up, until we let loose and feel we verbally have to rip into someone. This pressure cooker type of lifestyle systematically moves us farther and farther from our center cores and we begin to believe that chaos in our life is the norm.

Dropping the chaos and not picking it up again is a major milestone to lifting the mind fog. It is the simple awareness that we have the ability and choice to drop the chaos that will make us progressive.

4

THE EGO, NEUROSIS, COMPLAINING, AND OTHER FUN TOPICS

"THE SUN WILL SET WITHOUT YOUR ASSISTANCE."
-YIDDISH PROVERB

THE EGO

The ego is a trick we create to oppose our real selves. I usually refer to the ego as layers of nonsense. We create the beliefs that if we loose weight, color our hair, buy a newer car, have a bigger house that we will be happy. We could collect all the riches, have a facelift, travel to the four corners of the earth, and, afterwards, although we will have done a lot of things we still will not be happy. A lot of people live in a state of constant ego-driven mania. They become addicted to the things the world has to offer. The problem occurs because they constantly strive and collect these things.

47

The more we get, the more we want. As time goes on, we begin to put a higher percentage of our happiness into collecting possessions. Our society teaches us from an early age that we need hair so full it must bounce when we walk. The cars we drive now are part of our individual sex appeal. The TV commercials teach us that our jeans need to fit a specific way for us to be more appealing to each other. We really don't have to judge any of these things as bad or good, we just need to be aware that anything external is just that, external. The ego is the founder of "my," my boat, my car, my jewelry, my clothes, my house, my toys. We love to control all of these things. This control we think will make us happy. The ego is a fraud, it isn't who we really are despite the fact that we have designed and crafted it our entire life. The ego thrives on approval from others, including our spouses, our bosses, our parents, our friends. Please don't misunderstand, approval is great as long as we are aware that our happiness cannot ever come from outside forces.

Our true self is who we are at the very core of our being. Call it whatever label we want to, be it spirit or soul or inner guidance. When we are operating on this plane, we become fearless of challenges, criticism becomes no concern of ours, especially when the criticism is directed toward us. We will not have a need or desire to control others. This self power becomes permanent because we derive our powers from within, therefore it stays with us. We can't crash it, and it can't fall when the stock market does. There are many fringe benefits of operating from our core. We become totally peaceful with all of our decisions. We actually loose the need to second guess ourselves on anything. An incredible bonding with people becomes the norm. Everything aligns in a perfect order, and we look back and say, "Wow! That outcome is as fantastic as we'd ever imagined it could be."

Each and every one of us has this pure artesian well of creativity at the center of our being. By tapping into it we are stimulated to grow. As a result, it helps us to respect others and prevents us from feeling beneath or above anyone, or anything.

Everyone has experienced bits and pieces of this bliss. What we need to learn is to stay in that peacefulness. All we have to do is choose to do it. We choose to be depressed, sad, or happy. It can be said that those choices are so reflexive that they appear to be spontaneous and beyond our control. We so quickly choose depression that it appears to have come in on its own without our making a choice. Our personal growth comes when we realize that we and only we determine how long we stay in turmoil. When everything is synchronized, we attract people that somehow become the natural support for our desires. How ironic that we end up getting exactly what we want once we start operating from love rather than fear.

TAMING THE EGO

Out of control egos are self destructive, consequently, it only makes sense to practice keeping them under control. Ever since I was a child it has never bothered me to be alone. In fact, I could say I looked forward to it and still do. Bringing periods of silence into our lives help us to clear the mind fog. I have met people who even sleep with the radio or TV on because they feel they need a sense of others around. There are numerous ways to clear our slates, so to speak. Some folks like to walk on the beach and afterwards feel completely refreshed. Others close their eyes and listen to soft instrumental music. Some hike on mountain trails and some get what they need by sitting with their arms wrapped around their knees admiring the beauty of a mulberry tree. A tremendous unleashing of power becomes apparent. This crystal clear approach to thinking is the meaning of the word fulfillment. Another way to tame the ego is to stop making a game out of judging people. When we declare judgement on others, we say absolutely nothing about them but we sure say a lot about ourselves. Perhaps we can start our missions by deciding for the next 24-hour period we will not judge anything. If we don't like the dress our adult daughters wear, realize that it is their choice, not ours. If the waitress at the diner chews gum and calls us hon., be aware that a sarcastic comment on her behavior gains us nothing. This realization really hits at our "cores."

NATURES BEAUTY SOFTENS THE EGO

While vacationing in Alaska my wife and I visited a raptor center. This center started with a single idea by someone who wanted to help sick and injured eagles. The individual found an adult eagle helplessly hopping in the tall grass because it had an arrow through its wing. Other birds there have been shot or maimed by humans all because of mans' own self loathing. Over the years money has been donated for the purpose of maintaining these beautiful animals since they cannot survive in the wild. Most of the money is spent on education which helps the public to realize that these animals have a lot to offer--beauty. It is our natural state to be happy and to contribute to the world. The individual that had the fortitude, determination, and love for these birds affected more than the birds' lives.

Several thousand people go through the raptor center every year. We have an opportunity to see the birds from just a few feet away. We first notice the sharpness of the eyes, the innate confidence in the movements, and the distinct coloring of the feathers. The people that go through this center are struck with an appreciation and a desire to learn more about this living artwork we call an eagle.

NEUROSIS

To be neurotic is to never be content with the way our lives are going. The least little things will upset us, including all the things that we have no control over. A constant state of over analysis is really a form of mind violence. So many people live their lives in what I call a state of mild shock. They react to everything, and their entire life is spent catastrophizing. There is no question in my mind that worry and panic contribute to one's own illnesses. The endorphines that we emit on a cellular level do affect our bodies' chemistry. As more and more studies are completed they are showing us that the mind - body connection is very much related. Twenty years ago people who thought that the mind was more powerful than the body were considered quacks. Today a whole new psychology has resurrected because more and more people are willing to accept that there could be alternatives to their past thinking. Most people spend so much time treating their symptoms that it never occurs to them that the answers are all within their cores. It takes practice to remain aware so when we find that we are playing the same destructive tune over and over, we can remember to change the channel. It's our choice to live in chaos or a state of fulfillment. This life is too short to choose chaos. Often when I go out on a personal appearance through radio or TV on Saturday and Sunday afternoons people will make the statement that I must be incredibly tired. After all, "I have been up since 5:00 this morning, I've already done a three-hour radio show, TV segments, and now I have to meet all these people!" I always respond with the truth, "by meeting all of you fantastic people I not only learn more about my passion, plants, but I also become energized by the giving interaction." It's so true. It's the best job in the world, and my passion is expanded and I'm able to stimulate others' passions by just talking about what I love, growing plants.

Sharing of knowledge is a gift that we all can give to others on a daily basis. Everybody is a teacher because we all have different life experiences. When we start giving away our knowledge our center cores become more defined.

CHICKEN LITTLE

To live in a neurotic state is to live in panic. "It isn't going to work," neurotics say. "If it does work, something bad will happen." "We can't win for loosing." That's how neurotics talk all the time. They can't possibly focus on accomplishing anything because they're too caught up in the whirlwind. They always have a million things to do, grabbing a raincoat, they stand by the door looking out as if they are seeing rain for the first time in their lives. "My day is ruined. I'll never be on schedule." "I can't go out in this." Neurotics are masters of the word can't. I love what Henry Ford said: "If you think you can or you think you can't you're right." Perpetual worry plays a major role in holding us back. Every single thought that originates in our mind contributes to a negative or successful outcome. When negative thoughts or worries are compounded over and over again, the process feeds on itself. Remember, what we think about expands. Negativity is not a genetic thing. It is nothing more than a symptom of something going on in the deeper, thicker fog of our minds. Likewise, positive thoughts are just as powerful in a progressive sense. We're aware of it, and we're glad they're there. Oh, but don't be surprised. We put them there!

ASK OURSELVES?

Is it possible that we could be wrong? Most people see what they see, make a determination and decide that's the way it is, period. They are not willing to add any new information or details that could possibly interfere with the perception they have created, and finalized. As our consciousness expands, we become willing to "see" that there are several ways to "see" a situation. The perceived problem suddenly becomes smaller. Quite often it will even disappear. For this to work, we must be willing to accept the fact that we could be wrong about our present perceptions.

It all once again comes down to attitude. The thought process that we and only we develop translates into the nitty gritty details of our lives.

So the next time we start to build an emotional wall, between ourselves and our family, friends or co-workers we need to first place a mirror on the wall, stand firmly in the center and ask ourselves: Is it possible that we could be wrong?

By asking ourselves this question we become swashbucklers with our egos. It pays off though; the fog begins to clear and we realize that in fact, we are aware.

YOUR WINDOW TO THE WORLD MIGHT BE YOUR OWN FRONT DOOR

There is a country song that has that line in it and as Jackie Gleason used to say "How sweet it is." Most people live their lives always on their tiptoes trying to look into other people's lives or windows. "What do they have?" "They must have been given something I didn't get." "If I could find out what breaks they got, then I'll know the secrets." They are the people who can't watch "Lifestyles of the Rich and Famous" because they become angry and disgusted that someone has all those "things." This same person would love to have all those "things." The problem is that they can't lift their own mind-fog to be able to grasp those "things."

The secret is that there are no secrets. Loving thoughts help to reveal our true selves. It is the life inheritance that everybody wants and, ironically, everybody already has it. It's their own front door!

Negative thoughts will always compound more negative thoughts. If we indulge attack thoughts, whether they are subtle or bold, they totally block our best interest. Thoughts are like food for the mind. When we fill it with attack, judgement, and attachment, we get what we expect. When positive energy flows, everything is aligned. We deflect things that formally immobilized us and we continue to peddle steady.

All the great financial gurus like, Joe Burt, Jack Nelson, Don McDonald and others often talk about the benefits of dollar cost averaging. If we stick with it they say, keep making those routine deposits, the exponential growth will reward us. The same holds true for our thought systems.

COMPLAINING

In the third grade on the very first day of class, like all first days there was a lot of excitement. A new teacher, new clothes, new kids to make friends with, and I even had a new "Get Smart" lunch box! Oh, life was good. That's when it happened. The most exciting thing in my life suddenly appeared. I felt a tap on my shoulder and wow, there she was, the girl of my dreams. She had full shoulder length black hair, dimples so deep I could drown in them, and a smile so pretty I had to remind myself to breathe! "Hi, I'm Michelle. Do you think you could sharpen my pencil?" "Oh, sure," I jumped. "Do you just have one, I could do all of them in your school box if you like?" "No, one for now is fine," she said. A moment later I returned with the sharpest, most perfect pencil the education system has ever known.

As I slowly handed it to her, she once again smiled that smile, twitched her nose, batted her eyes, and shrugged her shoulders all at the same time. "Thank you," she said. This was it! I instantly began making plans for the end of the year. Beautiful Michelle could be the school princess and I could be the king. "Wow! what a team, I could sharpen her pencil all day and she could thank me with those adorable little smiles of hers." Life was good.

As the days grew on, I noticed that Michelle would find fault with the sharpness of the pencil. "It's just not right, the tip always breaks," she would complain. I willingly and affectionately did it over again and again and again. Then I noticed something else about Michelle. She found fault with everything that was occurring in school. She whined and complained to the teacher about anything and everything. She even got to the point where she would sigh just before she would begin yet another complaint. Her whining, complaining, and manipulating started that very first week of school and intensified.

One day our teacher decided that we were going to have a lesson in perception. She handed all of us that famous line drawing of the beautiful face of a young woman as well as the face of a witch. One would see whatever he or she saw depending on how he or she would look at the drawing. I first saw the beautiful face. My classmates all around me were saying things like, "Oh, cool it's a witch!" "What drawing did they get," I thought. Then I tilted my head and saw the witch too! My first judgement thought was to name the drawing Michelle, beautiful on the outside but certainly quite different upon closer examination. Throughout the year I continued to stay friends with Michelle, but I concluded that I certainly didn't need her as my princess. Michelle's whining got to the point where the teacher even noticed and other kids would often tell her to "just shut-up." Michelle loved all the attention and that's why her complaining intensified. I now saw her as a public irritant. By the end of the year I was so glad to move on because I couldn't wait to get away from the girl I thought was the girl of my dreams!

For the rest of elementary and middle school our paths never crossed. Then, in high school science class suddenly, she appeared. I didn't even recognize her physically, but that whine, the constant complaining gave her away. I knew that tone of voice and attitude. It all became so crystal clear. She never changed. Her form and body changed but her inner light bulb still was more like a bug zapper.

I concluded that there are a lot of Michelles in the world and they're always going to be there. I figured that it was her choice to operate from fear, and it was my choice not to take it as my fear. I studied. I played. I made friends with my classmates that were progressive and made a conscious decision to learn and grow. I decided that neither Michelle nor anyone else was going to draw me into their bug zapper.

CUTE TV

We need only to look at TV sitcoms to see that our society seems to think that complaints and sarcasms are cute. Which sitcom doesn't have a wise cracking, bushy haired kid that knows how to solve all the worlds' problems? The chronic complaining is often hybridized with a sarcastic intellect. Yes, it's right there every night for the world to see. TV is glorifying, complaining and sarcasm. It's epidemic. Everybody laughs. Some parents even use TV to babysit their children for hours on end. Of course, there are plenty of quality TV shows, too. It's like everything else. It comes down to our choice. We can choose to perpetuate the myth that the world is really like these TV sitcoms or we can choose to develop our own, original belief system.

DON'T CULTIVATE ANGER

A lot of people are like a sponge when it comes to anger. They love to absorb every single drop of someone else's anger. They are always able to succeed in finding it simply because they are always looking for it. When we operate from negativity that is what we find more of. That is what expands and becomes the driving force in our lives. When we allow the weeds to grow in the garden, they reseed. They get bigger, stronger and more deeply rooted. It is far easier to get rid of the weeds before they reseed, so they don't destroy the garden. Other people's anger is their own personal chaos, not ours. If we choose to take it on and join in their little hate circle of energy, we expand the problem. The solution will always be found in how we process the other person's anger.

Recently while waiting in line at an airport ticket counter dozens of people watched as a drama unfolded right before our eyes. It seems an entire family was late getting to the airport, and, although the scheduled time for the flight was still twelve or fifteen minutes away, the sales ticketer explained that all tickets had to be processed by a specific time which they just missed. Consequently, they would have to take another flight. Centered around this decision was a lot of loud verbal abuse from the family and lots of gesturing with their hands. The family moved onto the supervisor where the drama continued in a similar fashion. I was next in line and the sales ticketer angrily told me after examining my ticket that not only had I missed the flight, but I even had the wrong day of the flight! I calmly and softly pointed to the date and time of my ticket with my pen explaining to her that in fact my flight was leaving in one hour. She then put her hand on her mouth and mumbled something about the people in front of me. Her own mind-fog did not allow her to process the correct date or time of my flight. She was still hanging onto the drama that proceeded my appearance in her movie! I responded by smiling and squarely looking her in the eye and saying "Hey. Isn't it tough when someone drops all those marbles in our walkway?" She laughed and said, "Sir, I'm sorry I think that last scene was a cannon ball in my walkway, and I'm so sorry I aimed at you!" The myth was that the cannon ball had to be fired in the first place. Whether we become part of someone else's anger or are the original creator of it, doesn't matter. What matters is that we don't allow ourselves to jump into the circle of chaos. When we do, we lose our balance. Our entire thinking process becomes fogged, preventing us from functioning in a progressive peddle steady fashion.

MIND POLLUTION

Mind pollution is cumulative and is like an adding machine building on all the little perceived daily annoyances. When I was a kid starting my first year of algebra, I soon decided that I didn't like it, didn't want it, didn't need it, and consequently wasn't going to learn it. The professor might as well have had 6-6-6 A+B= "no way" imprinted on his forehead. In fact, I referred to him as the anti-teacher. He would mumble something to us that I never heard then would turn around and start writing all these numbers and letters on the blackboard. Oh, and it wasn't just one blackboard. He would fill two blackboards with all this hieroglyphics all the while mumbling while writing, never turning around. I never heard a thing he said. All I heard was the chalk quickly scratching on the blackboard. All the other kids around me seemed to do well. They nodded their head with every single equal sign. I soon realized that I had to redefine my goal. What was it that I wanted out of this class? Well, I decided that I needed to graduate. Therefore, I needed to pass. I immediately found a family friend who in fact was a math teacher who was willing to tutor me on her time off. She lived on the absolute other end of Fort Lauderdale in a congested part of town. Three days a week I got in my truck, paid my toll on the turnpike, waited in traffic, and 40 minutes later arrived at my tutor's house. She simplified algebra by breaking it into steps or phases and explained that I was going to learn a foreign language. She calmly explained it and when I didn't get it she calmly explained it again. Slowly but surely I began to increase my test scores. I was no longer late to class because I dreaded it. I simply acquired the basic skills I needed to get what I wanted. Sure, I had to jump through lots of hoops to get where I needed to be, but at the end I reached my goal. I passed. I didn't particularly pass with the proverbial flying colors, but I found a way to get what I wanted. Whether we take the short road or the long road ultimately will not prevent us from our goals. What will prevent us from peddling steadily is if we choose to take a detour and ride on the rocky, unterraced edge. Remember, the cliffs can be sharp and it simply isn't necessary to get off the path. We need to make a choice with the path we're going to take and as long as we peddle steadily we'll get where we want to go.

5

BALANCE

I'M ON THIS TEETER TOTTER AND I CAN'T GET DOWN

"ONE CANNOT MANAGE TOO MANY AFFAIRS; LIKE PUMPKINS IN THE WATER, ONE POPS UP WHILE YOU TRY TO HOLD DOWN THE OTHER."
-CHINESE PROVERB

HARMONY

In order to live in a state of bliss and contentment, we need to design our own personal, motivational system. We need to be willing to give up all of our judgements. Some people enjoy the perverse fun of putting others down. Their thinking is warped. They conclude that by attacking others they will put themselves up on a higher pedestal.

Synchroneity in our lives is what we all need to strive for. Synchroneity happens when every event falls into perfect harmony. For synchroneity to occur in a totally, positive

65

venue and continue to happen, we just need to be willing and be able to receive more of it. The more we accept, the more it will manifest itself in each and every moment of our lives.

When I was a child in Fort Lauderdale I started a nursery. As a teenager, I took forays to Central and South America, and all throughout the Caribbean, I collected exotic plants. Starting at the age of fifteen, I spent three summers in Costa Rica with an incredible loving progressive family that had a profound effect on my life. The Montealegres were a paradigm of what happens in one's life when a positive balance is conceived, realized, and accomplished.

Physically beautiful and intrinsically charming, they seemed to be counterparts of movie stars like Sophia Loren and Clark Gable. They were a family involved in politics, big business, charity, and social work. At 5:00 a.m. Rudolpho and I would leave the rambling estate and go to their sugar and coffee plantation. Rudolpho orchestrated the empire of several hundred workers from his office. I watched him as he dealt with his businesses as a great canoe ride. He worked hard but he also laughed and made his workdays fun. Later in the day, Carmen would pick me up and we would do something with their two children Lisa and Macho, the boy who was my exact age. Carmen often had personal responsibilities with various charities, and, like

Rudolpho, managed her day as a great adventure. I didn't speak their language, but they spoke broken English. Occasionally, Carmen would have trouble with a few English words and we laughed as I would try to figure out what she was saying. The great thing that I learned out of the summers there was that I did learn their language, but it wasn't Spanish. I learned that you can work hard, accomplish what you want, and have a great time doing it. Often in the evenings, the Montealegres threw elaborate parties. I met fascinating people from all over the world, including political leaders, sports stars and even princesses. They treated everyone that crossed their path as a special friend.

THE PARTY

Carmen and Rudolpho designed a masterpiece of an estate. The 10,000 plus square foot home was cantilevered into the side of a mountain. Open air architecture and Mexican tiles throughout, antiques, and hand crafted pieces from Spain were abundant. Carmen's family was from Spain, originally, and she was proud of her heritage and shared the stories of the beautiful artwork with me. We had lots of family and friend barbeques. I noticed a pattern beginning to develop. All of Carmen and Rudolpho's friends were very much like them. They all had exuberance and a zest for life! I took to this environment like a duck to water. I shook hands and mingled and talked to a mixture of personalities unlike anything I had ever experienced before. I saw that successful people who had many material things had a seemingly flawless balance in their lives. They had friends; they had laughter; they had the sun in the morning, and the moon at night! All of these people were involved with successful businesses but their main goal was to make a contribution. They were active in national and world charities and it was obvious to me that their giving and loving attitudes payed great dividends in their personal lives.

THE BUSINESSMAN

At one of the Montealegre's parties I met a businessman, who in a simple conversation, taught me the "rule" of putting back into the world more than you take. As we were served homemade chocolate-covered ice cream bars, we talked about the architecture and beauty of Carmen and Rudolpho's home. We sat in soft, tropical, wicker chairs on the columned, tiled veranda and looked out upon all the beauty. The pool was in our foreground with original boulders that were incorporated into the water. The landscape was a tall lush tropical mountain planted with variegated bananas, heliconias, exotic prayer plants and cascading Philodendron verocosum, that had a heart-shaped leaf that resembled a church's stained glass. A waterfall just left of the center created soothing sounds as it tumbled into the deep end of the pool. The gentleman shared with me the details of the house and he explained that the same water from the fall meandered throughout the various, ponds, fountains, and landscapes outside the home as well as inside. The water flowed to the foyer down a stunning indoor rock wall planted with ferns, bromeliads, and flowering anthuriums the size of dinner plates growing on the rocks! From there the water flowed outside to a stream at the edge of the property. I explained to the man my intentions and goals of growing plants and I told him how Carmen would take me to the area nurseries and anthurium farms so that I could study and collect unusual species. He listened with great interest, asking questions and gaining more knowledge along the way. He seemed to think I had an exciting future planned and very much encouraged me to continue on my life's path. He didn't volunteer the type of work he did, so curiosity allowed me to ask plenty of questions. He explained that he was in the timber business as well as several others, but timber was his main passion. He had thousands of acres and proceeded to tell me about the nuances of growing trees. He was dogmatic in making the point that whatever he harvested he would triple the volume of new plantings. He explained that the new trees probably wouldn't even be harvested in his lifetime but he had an inner guidance to replant for the future. Years earlier he purchased acreage with old, existing native timber, and his eyes sparkled as he talked about how he was developing it, not to be clear cut for business purposes, but instead as a park with nature trails for fun and educational purposes. He talked to me about having a mission or life purpose and his theme was consistent--be passionate and do more than just put back what you use. He used words like contribution and love and abundance. I mentioned to him that with all the material things he has achieved that he didn't act like he was better than anyone else. He replied that he wasn't better or any worse. He was just going with his gut in everything he did. He felt that nature gave us a gut instinct to use and he believed that we had to develop it to make a contribution to the world. He was the opposite of self absorbed. He wasn't concerned about what other people thought. He just played to his own drum beat. Later, I had the pleasure of meeting his charismatic and charming wife, and Carmen explained to her that we were taking forays to nurseries as well as to the jungle. She, like her husband took the time to encourage me and sincerely commented that she knew I had an exciting, fun-filled life ahead of me. I mentioned to her that the first fifteen years had been quite eventful and exciting and I couldn't wait to see what would happen in the next fifteen years. I'll never forget what she said in closing, "Hey. You've contributed and appreciated so much in fifteen years, you are already doing the ultimate. It's going to continue."

Chance meetings with people like that solidified my confidence and sure enough the next fifteen years were just as good. Rudolpho later explained to me that the lady I was talking with was the president of a world hunger foundation and active with many other contributing charities. I also learned that she owned and operated many hotels. She was a mover and shaker just like her husband and just like all the other friends of the Montealegres. This couple took the time to show a sincere interest in my young life. Their simple words of encouragement gave me a lot of motivation. Throughout the years I have always made a special point to provide a definite balance in my life. I have since realized that my coincidental meeting with this couple that shinned so brightly to me with balance in their life was not just an ordinary coincidence. I have realized that the universe knows exactly what it's doing!

THE LITTLE DRUMMER BOY KNOWS WHICH SIDE IS UP!

In the classic Christmas carol the little drummer boy already had everything that he needed. He had nothing to give the king, at least nothing tangible. He had no precious jewels and no money but he willingly gave the king what he had -- all he had, his song on the drum. He gave his gift out of his heart and it sparkled brighter than any jewel ever could.

There is a great lesson in that carol. Maybe we are not in a financial position to offer money to charity. Maybe we don't have material things to donate. None of that stuff is necessary for us to make a contribution to others. We could do what my friend Jane Freer does, volunteer our services to the hospital. We could bake a cake for a friend or a neighbor. We could root some cuttings from our poinsettia to be given as Christmas gifts or we could simply write a poem to someone we care about. Sometimes people who get depressed don't have a clue with what to do with their life. If we listen to them talk, everything centers around them. They are the world's victims in their minds. The answer for them is to do anything rather than peddle backwards. That something I'm referring to has everything to do with helping others.

BALANCE IS A CHOICE

If we are immobilized by our thoughts, we are no longer in a state of growth but a state of stagnation or perhaps we're even peddling backwards. The answer is in our choice. Anything that prevents us from functioning or getting the things we want or doing the things we want to do and care about is a choice that we make. We make the choice to live the way we want to live. We can choose chaos or we can function in peace and see results.

Once we start making excuses for ourselves, we need to remind ourselves that they are only excuses to back peddle. We have all known people in school that were like superpeople. They looked great; they were physically in shape; they were good at sports, and, as if that's not enough, they even made great grades. What these people had were great attitudes. They expected all of these great things and that's exactly what they got.

Our friend Maggie Maney would often suggest that Nalini and I vacation at the beach. We explained that after working in the sun all day, we really didn't feel like baking in the sun like a potato. We had no desire to do that. Maggie had a wonderful answer, "Don't allow the sun to stop you from enjoying the beach. Remember that you can enjoy the beach early in the morning before it gets hot. You can enjoy it at twilight as the sun goes down and at night the ocean sounds are such an incredible invigoration!" It's true there is a lot to walking barefoot in the sand and enjoying the beach at other times other than when the sun is out.

HIGHLIGHTING OUR OWN ABILITIES

Let's say we had a goldplated dinner plate that was an antique given to us by our grandmother. Let's say that it was valuable to us monetarily, artistically, and sentimentally. We would not abuse this artifact. We would do everything we could to highlight it and to observe it and to continue to enjoy its beauty for the rest of our lives. Well, that's the way we have to think about ourselves. We have to always be able to grow and highlight our own abilities, knowledge, and artistic talents. We can do this by being honest with ourselves and by making a commitment to go after what we want. Every human being is unique and it is clear non-fogged thinking that helps us to realize this. There is always a way for us to get what we want. For example, if it is a specific type job we want we need to plan the necessary route to get it. Once we plan, we must stay on the path.

STAYING ON THE PATH

We find that fully functioning people have goals and missions to help attain what they want out of life. These people do not have a need to explain to others why they do certain things. They have no need for other people to approve or disapprove what they do. They choose to do what makes sense to them in how they lead their daily lives. Other people's opinions should have nothing to do with how we choose to live our lives.

PERCEPTION

Peoples' perceptions are only what they think. They're not what you think. In my case, people listen to my radio show or see the TV segments and may decide that I'm good or bad. I know that I have no control over what they think. Really, what they think doesn't have anything to do with me. Peoples' opinions reflect only their own perceptions. One time on the radio show, "The Garden Rebel," I had some things to say about the Chinese tallow tree. I detailed the beauty and benefits of the tree then proceeded to take calls. The next week I received two letters in the mail. The first one's opening line was, "How could you promote such a dangerous tree?" The letter was from the president of the Native Plant Society and was without a doubt the most hateful letter I had ever received. She proceeded to explain that this tree was not a native. "It has no intrinsically good qualities and because of its aggressive habit, it chokes and kills our native vegetation." She quoted a line in an article she sent on how there was a cluster of these trees spotted along the turnpike near Gainesville, Florida. In a period of three years this cluster had grown into a mass of ten or twelve trees. "It could potentially kill out our palmettos and scrub oaks that birds love!" she exclaimed. I just happen to know that the palmetto is perhaps the most common plant in the South and besides I also know that birds didn't prejudge Chinese tallows. In fact, from what I could tell, birds loved them! I noticed that the remainder of the article had a political feel about it. It slandered any plant that wasn't a native. "They're not adapted here. They just bring more pests and eventually will die out!" Clearly, the article was not willing to accept any foreign species as beneficial. I noticed that the article was written by the proprietor of a nursery that specialized in native plants. His agenda was to belittle the items he did not sell. I thought it was sad that some people would have to prejudge a showy, exotic species that had so much to offer.

The second letter was bursting with

compliments. It was loaded with exclamation points, but it came from a totally different "core." The lady in the letter explained how she perked up when she heard me sing the praises of the Chinese tallow. She loved its habit of growth, its heart-shaped leaf and especially loved the way it turned bright yellow and orange in the fall. She proceeded to write that she had been gardening her entire life and that few trees give her the enjoyment that her Chinese tallow does. For seven years she was able to watch the birds feed and play in the tree. She under planted it with hybrid daylilies and blue lilies of the Nile which accented it even more. "Mr. Sims," she said, "I have a small backyard and it fits back there as if God planted it himself." She was right. He did.

IF I KNEW THE DIFFERENCE BETWEEN GOOD ADVICE AND BAD, I WOULDN'T NEED ADVICE

If we go to someone and ask them for advice, we shouldn't blame them if the situation doesn't work in our favor. We asked for the advice. We internalized it and made the final decision. We responded with what we felt was our own best ability to make the decision at the time. We chose the person who gave us the advice and we made the decision to do what we wanted to do. We might as well could have chosen not to follow the advice. Accepting responsibility for our own actions is a sign of human growth.

As we become more centered, we make choices in our lives that originate from a knowing-type of attitude rather than a lets try this-type of attitude. When this happens our self-esteem rises and we continue to build confidence that we are making the right choices. It's all part of the growing process.

DR. TONY PREVITE

Tony has been a good lesson for me in regard to balance in my life. As an emergency room physician, he sees and has seen about everything there is to see. If he chose to make excuses about the world going to hell in a hand basket, he certainly would have lots of stuff to cite. He doesn't do that. He spends his work days energizing his patients. He sincerely gives to his patients his "take" on their situation and he sees to it that they get attention and care to the best of his ability.

I had not seen or heard from Tony in more than twelve years and wasn't even sure if the last address I had for him was correct. I wrote him a note but didn't hear back from him. Months went by and still no word from Tony. Then one day I took a day off to catch up on some odds and ends at the nursery. I casually looked up and saw a lady and a man smiling and walking towards me. I didn't recognize them. Then suddenly a voice said, "Vince, it's Tony!"

"Wow. It's great to see you."

"This is my wife, Kerri."

"What are you doing?" I asked.

"Well, we came to see you and were just driving through Florida. Our philosophy is wherever we end up is where we're supposed to be."

I was delighted so I replied, "You've ended up here for the next few days. This is perfect. You can stay at my father's new house at the front of the property. He doesn't move in until next week."

For the next several hours we got caught up on each other's lives. His wife was just as fun and energized and we spent the afternoon hitting golf balls from the edge of my property line. Later we went out to a Japanese restaurant and had a fantastic dinner and conversation. Tony and Kerri see their free time as totally timeless. They don't set time limits or put rules, parameters, or restrictions on their doings. "We're on time and correctly where we should be wherever we are. It's for us to discover and appreciate the meaning of the moment in which we find ourselves."
I love the attitude. They are not restricted by what other people may or may not think. They believe that what counts is that they do what makes sense to them. As a hobby, Tony writes poetry and screen plays. Tony has chosen the pen name Noah Herald. One night at dinner, Tony explained that he just finished writing yet another screen play. "You're kidding" I said, as he proceeded to tell me the hilarious plot and detailed some of the characters. "Where is it?" I asked. "It's out there," Tony replied. "What do you mean? Have you sent it out to lots of Hollywood producers?" I asked. "No, Vince. It's just out there." "Out where, Tony?" "Just

out there in the universe," he said again. "I mailed it to some of my friends and family. I have no intention or desire to benefit from it monetarily. I just wanted them to enjoy it." "But, Tony, someone could steal it, duplicate it, and show it to millions of people and make a lot of money from it." "I hope so Vince. That's the whole idea. That's the whole idea." Then Tony replied, "For me, writing a screen play is like raising a child as well as I know how. You write the play as well as you know how then send it out in the world confident that it will find its way and come into its own."

I'M ON THIS TEETER TOTTER AND I CAN'T GET DOWN

The problems that we collect and hold onto as if they have values are what makes the other end of the teeter totter so heavy. We can stack the baggage in suitcases and load one right on top of the other. One suitcase could be labeled work; another, money problems; another, family problems; and another, negative thoughts. Until we stop packing our suitcases with energies that hold us back and weigh the teeter totter down, we can't stop dangling our feet in helplessness. We need to only pack the things that we're going to always use that can help us. Our suitcases should be filled with things we give away to others, things we love, things that serve us rather than harm us.

My friend Stacy McPherson is a sales executive with WDBO radio in Orlando. Her job is action packed, as she works with on air personalities, business clients and co-workers. She is one of the hardest working people I know, and what she works the hardest at is further developing her relationship with people. She studies and understands the principles of teamwork and knows that when it's all working together great positive progress results. She often has to put together deals that satisfy all the parties involved, ie, her bosses (that's important), her clients (that's important), and her coworkers (that's important). Occasionally, like everyone else's workday something might go wrong that interferes with her expected outcome. When that happens she says, "Vince, my instinct is to get in there and fight and control the problem. If I find myself building up like a volcano, I now take deep breaths and walk away from the situation. I go back to it when I'm calm and ready to see the situation from a different angle." Stacy's positive outlook is the reason she loves what she does and is considered one of the best sales executives in the radio industry.

6

WAKE UP AND SMELL THE TEA OLIVES

"THE SUN SHINES BRIGHTER AFTER A SHOWER."
-YIDDISH PROVERB

Osmanthus fragrans, also known as the Tea Olive are plants that do not have the showiest, most beautiful foliage in the world. They don't particularity have an attractive habit of growth, usually growing thin and spindly. What they do have, however, is the softest, most gentle, relaxing fragrance, that rivals a flawless gardenia. Once we realize that they have this attribute, we ignore or forget all the things that the plant doesn't have. That's the way the canoe ride through life is. There are lots of things that are judged to be valueless, but after closer examination it's discovered that, in fact, not only are they worthy, they're unique! A single idea or thought can have such an incredible kick start to one's life. Like everything else, success is all in the attitude. So many people go through their entire life "sleeping," never bothering to take the step to become progressive. Now is that special time to "Wake Up and Smell the Tea Olives!"

R-U-on-E?

We all have reached the breaking point. We all have been depressed. Each and every one of us has at one time or another felt we were in a big black hole and couldn't crawl out. External circumstances happen, and we have to deal with them and sometimes, when we're really tested, an avalanche of problems occurs simultaneously. Most of the time we can dig ourselves out, but sometimes we need help. Help can be from a good friend, neighbor, church or charity. One of the most inspirational people I've ever met is a man named Tony Georgio. Tony is an unpretentious man married to an unpretentious lady named Lauren. Tony goes about his daily life as a man on a mission. He lives in a subdivision and gardens and works as a bellman at a theme park hotel. His work shift varies from day to evening. He sincerely greets people daily with a smile. Tony dedicates all of his spare time to the Compassion Children's Foundation which he and his wife created. The foundation isn't loaded with money. It isn't housed in a mirrored skyscraper. In fact, it's in a small office down a long hallway in a small church.

He doesn't have expensive office equipment but what he does have was donated by people who cared. The foundation doesn't have a paid staff. In fact, Tony and his wife Lauren are the staff. The two of them simply truck along making a difference in the world. Tony decided to help people in need, and, even though it may be only one or two at a time, he has really made a dramatic difference in many people's lives. This is evidenced by the people he's helped. Tony's purpose began when his neighbor's 1 1/2 year old toddler was diagnosed with cancer. Insurance did not cover the preexisting condition and medical bills depleted everything the family had. Tony made a conscious decision right then and there to raise money to help the baby get the treatment he needed. The hospital needed more money if treatment was to continue. The hospital told the parents that the cancer was a rare form of leukemia, which children rarely get, subsequently, they did not have a protocol to follow. The hospital administration and doctors told the parents that even if they had the money there was only a 10% chance that their baby would survive. Tony wanted that family to have that 10% chance. By the time the family was told the pessimistic news, they had already lost their car and their house was in the stage of foreclosure. The mother had to quit work in order to tend to the needs and special care of her baby. The father was about to lose his gas station until Tony called the Texas oil company who supplied him and got an extension on his payments. Tony then called the television and radio stations, and even went on talk shows. He called the newspapers and the neighbors and anybody else that would listen. Tony along with the help of the community raised the money to help the baby through car washes and spaghetti dinner fund raisers. How did he do it? He wasn't a professional fund raiser. He wasn't a public speaker. He wasn't an independently wealthy man who had time on his hands. He was and is just a man who saw a problem and tried to solve it. His wife was there with him every inch, every small step of the way. Together, they do all the loads of federal and state paperwork for the foundation. They work long hours, and they do it with love and devotion not expecting any personal gain monetarily. People like Tony and his wife make a big contribution to the world. They do it with love and they do it well. They believe in their actions and their actions determine their results. By the way, the little boy, the little boy with only a 10% chance of survival, the little boy whose parents were told to spend his last days with him at home, is doing great! He's now 13 years old and completely cured.

Tony Georgio didn't allow a bureaucracy or a doctor's conclusion to dictate another person's future. Tony had a passion and a belief that life, any life is worthy, regardless of how advanced a disease was said to have been. For Tony his business is a people business, helping people. I think you'll agree he's mastered it.

Tony always needs volunteers and supporters. Here's the address and all contributions are tax deductible.

Compassion Children's Foundation
250 S.W. Ivanhoe Boulevard, Suite A
Orlando, Florida 32804

CHILDREN ARE SOME OF OUR BEST TEACHERS

When I watch my son, Dcota, play, he goes all out. He runs as fast as he can. He squeals and screams indeterminately in delight. He jumps over toys. He falls to his knees in the sand, gets dirt in his socks and on his face, and sweats like a billy goat on a hot August day. He isn't concerned about his clothes or his looks, his sole goal is to have fun and enjoy. He smiles and laughs and when I chase him, instantly I'm transformed into a fun loving, knee slapping kind of a guy. It shows me that the best way to learn and grow is to unlearn all of the conditioned thoughts that tend to hold us back in our daily lives. Play with a kid, any kid, the first chance you get. It's an opportunity to smile and laugh and appreciate the value in living.

SEIZE THE MOMENT

We have all heard the expression that we need to live in the moment. This is not just a clever contemporary phrase but rather a very powerful lifestyle. It is a myth to believe that bliss will come at a particular dated moment in the future. Some people see their youth and middle age years as a drudgery. The thing that makes it all worthwhile is the belief that when they retire, they can begin really living their life. How ironic that they feel that they need to live two thirds of their life before they feel they can be happy. Interacting with other people at work is something necessary for most of us. If we always look for problems in our chosen work, we are guaranteed to find them. Even if we change work, a whole new cast of characters to judge will instantly be there. Even if we perceive a character in our workplace to be a villain, in another workplace, another villain will appear, as long as we continue to blame others for our lot in life. No one person or idea or bureaucracy or system can hold us back. We are the sole determining factor that creates our own limitations.

KATHERINE I

As a young boy I started planting seeds and plants in soup cans. My neighbors saved me their cans, and later I purchased for three cents, one gallon size tomato paste cans from my elementary school kitchen. Soon I had quite a variety of plants and was in the nursery business. Shady Ridge nursery grew and became quite prosperous right there in my own backyard. There was an indoor plant section and a landscape plant section, a special spot for orchids and bromeliads and numerous tables set up with exotic plants that I had collected in Costa Rica, Honduras, and the Caribbean. I planted Australian tree ferns that grew so tall I could walk under them. It became my own oasis and I loved every minute of being outside.

One day while I was dividing bromeliads a wonderful smiling grey-haired lady drove up in a baby blue Cadillac. I'll never forget it. "Hi," she exclaimed! "I'm Katherine. I've been looking for you and I've heard about all the wonderful things you've done with plants." She explained that everybody calls her Katherine I "because, my last name is Isgette and no one can say it or spell it." An hour went by in about five minutes or so, it seemed. We chatted and laughed and became instant buddies.

Katherine invited me over to see the

gardens that she created for more than 30 years. I made arrangements to go see her the next day. What a delight her garden was. As my truck entered beyond the large wooden gates, I could immediately see that this was no ordinary landscape. There was a long curved driveway leading up to another set of gates. The gates were metal and had an oriental flare about them. Both sides of the drive were lushly landscaped with bird of paradises, Bolivian sunsets, bromeliads, and terrestrial orchids. Each species was grown to perfection, it seemed. There were giant boulders on the edge of a lake with colorful, undulating flower beds around them. As I got out of my truck and opened the gate I was in total awe of my surroundings. As I walked towards the house that was surrounded by trees and palms and ferns, I can vividly remember thinking " I have heard of paradise and this is it." Katherine greeted me at the door with a big smile and proceeded to give me the tour of the estate. The outdoor garden areas were divided up into "rooms." There was one area in particular that was among my favorites. A small wooden carved sign said "the rainforest" at the entrance. A narrow, mulched path meandered along a black lagoon, a tree-fern forest was planted on a slope. The lagoon was bordered with various specimens of bamboos as well a blooming lobster claw gingers, and blue lilies of the Nile.

The whole scene seemed prehistoric to me. Except for the birds that chattered like kids on a playground, silence pervaded.

Each section of the vast tropical rainforest that Katherine had created over time had its unique personality and beauty. As we walked through the various curved paths, I would comment on a particular exotic species, and she would tell me about its history. Her enthusiasm and passion for the plants were contagious. She never tired of talking about plants and decided years earlier that her living environment was always going to be surrounded by beauty.

As the years went by, Katherine became "Grandma Kate" to me. She told me that she never really liked the name Kate but somehow when I said it, "it just seemed right." She enjoyed every moment out in her yard. At night she would sometimes go outside with a flashlight to see if one plant or another was blooming. Her garden was her love and relaxation. It was also a place to entertain friends and family, and she often donated its use for charity events. When one part of the garden became overgrown, she would figure out a new design and rebuild it, starting with new species that she had purchased or collected in a foreign country.

Grandma Kate certainly was one of the most inspirational people I've ever met. The thing I remember most often is that she always

91

took the time to enjoy the garden. She would sit and feed the black swans and the woodducks at the edge of the pond. She would slice mangos under the shade of a black olive tree. She admired the sunrises as well as the sunsets. She would leave corn on the cob out for the wildlife. Katherine felt that all wildlife was very much a part of the ecosystem and needed to be appreciated and not scolded. The way she lived her life was a very good series of lessons for me. Her life, like her garden bloomed and prospered. She welcomed change with open arms, and cultivated happiness everywhere she went. She stopped to smell the tea olives along each path of her life.

SUCCESSFUL WINNERS

By working in private business as well as the media of print, radio and television, I've had the opportunity to meet a variety of successful people. All of the people that have graciously contributed to the following pages all have a common denominator. They all have loving families; they all chose their work because they have a passion for it; and they all contribute to the community. Oh, and by the way, just like you and me, they all have problems that erupt from time to time.

Somehow, they successfully manage to maintain a balance in their life by doing what they want to do by enjoying all the benefits and opportunities that life has to offer. I found it fascinating to learn how successful people who are regarded as the best in their chosen profession all have a customized approach to lifting the mind fog. Despite the fact that they have some of the most stressful jobs in the world; every one of these winners still finds a way to become centered. I'm proud of my friends and all of them are a constant flowing well of inspiration for me. The following pages will help you see how winners lift the mind fog.

MARK BREWER

MANAGEMENT CONSULTANT

My Respite From The Journey

The day dawns cool and crisp by Florida standards. The blaze in the eastern sky explodes into a beautiful sunrise. Streaming orange and rust shards topped by smoky, gray caps remind me of dawn in the Appalachian mountains. The dew smells like fresh pine, and a wafting breeze cools the building perspiration on my forehead.

Suddenly, the sound of a horn drags me back to reality. It's a Ford passing my left side a little closer than I might like, the driver obviously surprised to be sharing this dark ribbon of asphalt with a two legged animal. I'm not in the mountains, but rather on a run through my southwest Orlando neighborhood.

My body feels free and powerful as I run through the darkness combining the two best forms of rejuvenation: aerobic exercise for the heart and guided imagery for the soul. As my speed increases, my heartbeat slows to a steady pace and my stride shifts to auto-pilot. Now, my mind takes over and transports me to wherever I want to be. As I run, ideas begin to come quickly, solutions for problems that cloud my senses are suddenly clear, and strategies for many baffling challenges flood over me.

Henry David Thoreau's writings first introduced me to an enlightening theory: "Life is a journey, not a destination." Yet, I see people around me who seem to focus more on winning the right job, buying the right house or car, or winning the lottery than they do living life at it's best. Thoreau preached that at the top of every mountain there is . . . another mountain, an experience we've all had. So, I try to remember to concentrate on the journey; being the best I can be and enjoying all the steps. I never take my eye off the destination, but I also never forget that strategy is no good without the right tactics.

Whether I'm hiking in the clear mountain dawn or running through city traffic, I get relief from the stress of everyday life through focused concentration. The release comes from letting my body do what it was designed to do . . . move. As my muscles concentrate on the struggle at hand, my mind is free to wander any trail I like.

After several days on the trail, when the routine of everyday life disappears, and you begin to focus on the journey of the hike, the realization comes that putting one foot in front of the other is both an art and a science. The perfection of doing it right reminds you that the journey of life is always more important than the destination. A thirty-mile hike or a ten-mile run requires that you put one foot in front of the other several thousand times. The more you do it the better, and less painful the experience is. Soon speed and endurance increase and you begin to feel the power and control that come when you are in shape to tackle the journey, any journey. The destination is always in the future.

WILLIAM DRYBURGH

FIRE CHIEF

When I am asleep, the troubles of the day and those that await me vanish for those precious few hours; but night gives way to day and that which is forgotten is remembered.

During the course of my day, time becomes my enemy. So many days I have had to tell my secretary that there is never enough time in the day to get everything accomplished.

The time it takes me to go from my home to my office is about eighteen minutes depending on the lights. I could spend this time listening to mindless chatter of disc jockeys and the playing of songs with words I can't understand, or I can use this time to my benefit. In my car alone with the windows up and the radio off; I am free of life's distractions that will feed on me when I arrive at my office like a piranha in a cheap Tarzan movie.

My car becomes my personalized think tank, and the pressures that created my mind fog melt away like the morning mist. I arrive at my destination confident that this day will be a great one.

97

CHER DUCKWORTH

RADIO PERSONALITY / PHOTOGRAPHER

Clearing the fog has changed throughout the years. There was once a time when a hot bubble bath, complete with lit candles and a glass of wine, worked well. Maybe that hot bath doesn't have the impact it once did. Perhaps because, back then, I was single, living in Houston and I only had twenty minutes to unlock my brain and cool my jets. It was nearly fail-proof.

While living in Los Angeles, clearing the fog meant a run around the high school track after work. On the weekends, a day at the beach was most beneficial. Not only did it clear the fog, it was always good for a suntan.

The year I spent living in the San Francisco Bay area was always made better by a trip down to Fisherman's Wharf, via the Bay Area Rapid Transit (BART), the trolley was good for a full day of fog clearing. Sometimes it got expensive, especially if I bought something I didn't need. Spending money seemed to work well with clearing any kind of fog.

Now, I'm married and live in sub-rural America. My brain needs more clearing than ever before. Today I find myself hanging out in the barn more and more. I've discovered a calming-of-the-senses when I convince my horse, Hope, brushing her is something she needs. Most of the time I just need to touch this twelve hundred pound animal and feed her carrots or apples. It's her choice to be next to me. OK, so her inspiration is a carrot. To her I might as well be wearing a sign that says "food," she nickers and whickers at me only because she thinks I might have something for her to eat. But that's OK, there's a back-to-basic perception that works very well. Hanging out in the barn keeps Hope groomed and keeps my mind clear.

PAUL DUCKWORTH

PROGRAM DIRECTOR
WDBO RADIO

As I sit at my official radio Program Director's desk, clumsily pecking away on my computer keyboard, I realize that the pressure is beginning to take its toll. "The opinions do not reflect those of the radio station or it's APPETIZERS," I have written. Yes, I know that I should have written ADVERTISERS, but I'm simply not functioning on all cylinders. It must be that dreaded MIND FOG. Is it the long hours? The doctor said eight hours of sleep is enough. He does mean eight hours a week, right? Perhaps, the incessant ringing of the phone has gotten to me. Don't get me wrong, I love hearing from listeners whose opinions of my station are well thought out and eloquently articulate. If only they would call me today. Instead, I'm hearing from listeners who feel compelled to blame me for the price of coffee, the Yankees faltering pitching, and the fact that Susan Lucci didn't win again. Regardless, of the cause, I'm in the MIND FOG.

So what do I do to clear that fog? I take a trip. No, not literally. I simply visit the travel agency in my mind. I may revisit a place that I've been before. Or, perhaps, I take a trip to a place of which I've only dreamed. I can't tell how often I return to that cruise ship bound for Alaska. I can see the massive sculptures of snow and ice and the spectacular signs of God's creation. I can feel the warmth of friendship of those with whom I shared this trip. And most of all, I get lost in the memories of the endless supply of food. You know, that buffet is a little bigger every time I think about it.

I may escape the mind fog, with a trip to beautiful Poipu Beach on the island of Kaui. No, I've never been there. But that doesn't matter. I've got cable. And that's enough information for a wonderful vacation in my mind.

Well, if you'll excuse me, it's the phone. But, don't worry, I can handle it. Because when that MIND FOG rolls in, my next stop is a ski chalet in the Swiss Alps. Wanna come?

PATRICIA N. FISHER

HIGH SCHOOL TEACHER

As a teacher in a typical American high school of the 90's, I continually find myself lost in the fog of everyday routine. Sixteen and seventeen-year-old students are a challenge, and more often than not, I find myself swept up in the tides of teenage emotion. Added to this are my own personal life experiences: a new marriage, a new grand baby, an aging father, and my responsibilities to myself. All of these things sometimes make my life overwhelming, and soon I find the fog has rolled in, and I am lost. When I am lost and confused and overwhelmed and pressured and stressed, I race. My thoughts tumble one upon another adding to my confusion. My pulse and heart rate accelerate. The more I do, the more there is to do. I speed out of control. How can I find my way through to peace once again?

One way for me to begin to clear the fog is to breathe, breathe consciously and slowly. This has immediate impact. I recall one momentous classroom confrontation. A young girl, full of anger and venom, began to rage at me during English class. She spoke loudly, declaring in blunt terms what she, her mother, and her boyfriend would do to me, and what she thought of my teaching abilities. My insides boiled, and anger flashed. I wanted to defend myself and attack her, but I knew that I had to follow procedure. Before I could send her from the room, I had to write up a referral that explained her behavior. As I walked to the desk to get a referral, I remembered to breathe. I focused on my breathing, deliberately slowing it down and attending to it. As I did this, calmness settled upon me. I still heard the girl, but it was as if she was in a movie that I observed. Continuing to focus on my breaths, I got the referral, filled it out, and sent her from the room. Throughout the entire incident, I spoke not a word to her. The rest of my students sat in stunned silence. After she left, I resumed my lesson, calmly and peacefully. Later on, several students told me how impressed they had been with the way that I handled the situation. I'd like to think that I taught another lesson besides English that day. Remembering to breathe and to slow down can help anyone leave the fog of anger for serenity and peace.

Speaking of serenity, the Serenity Prayer is another tool that I use to escape the fog of confusion. Most of us know it: "God, grant me the serenity to accept the things I cannot change, the courage to change the things that I can, and the wisdom to know the difference." The Serenity Prayer reminds me to put the focus on me and not on outside agents or events in my life. It also helps me

103

realize that the only thing in the world I can change is me. I cannot control my spouse, my daughters, my boss, the political arena, the weather, or prices. The only thing that I have total responsibility over is me. Once I learn to accept this, life becomes easier, and the fog lifts. Acceptance and change is not the easiest thing for me to do. I heard once that change is easy; resistance to change, painful. So it is. The Serenity Prayer sums up these ideas about living. When I am confused, if I can look objectively on my life and see what needs changing, I usually find that it is I. If I am upset because my spouse leaves his clothes on the floor, I can do either one of two things: I can accept his behavior and leave the clothes on the floor, or I can accept his behavior and pick them up. I will never be able to change him. Only he has the ability to change himself. I can choose to become upset and get trapped in the fog of complaining, arguing, and resenting, or I can remember the Serenity Prayer and accept the differences between my spouse and me. When I follow the simple task of saying and acting on the Serenity Prayer, I do not stay in the fog for long.

Both breathing and acting on the Serenity Prayer do much to restore my sanity. However, my favorite way of getting out of the confusion fog, I learned from *A Course in Miracles,* published by the Foundation for Inner Peace. This book contains lessons in spiritual

104

psychotherapy, lessons that have helped me immeasurably. From *A Course in Miracles* I have learned to ask my Higher Power to help me to see the world or situation or person differently. The world and the events in it are only figments of my perception, and, whenever I am upset, it is because I view the world as an upsetting place. The clearest example of this involves yet another teaching situation. Several years ago I had a student. I will call him John. It seemed that John's task in life was to make my life miserable. He succeeded. Daily I found myself dreading his appearance in class. By early winter, I knew that I had to do something. I tried all of the regular methods of discipline: phone calls home, detentions after school, referrals to the office. Nothing seemed to work. I talked this over with another student of *A Course in Miracles*. She suggested I use a technique taught by the *Course*. That night, during my evening prayers, I asked my Higher Power to help me see John differently, to change my perception. Then I forgot about it. The next morning, the bell rang for third hour class. Along came John. When I saw him, I knew my inside feelings were different. I felt no animosity toward him. He greeted me with a warm, open smile. From that day forward, the relationship between John and me was healed. My perception of him had changed, and where hate had been, love flowed. Ever since that time, whenever I have difficulty with a person or event , I ask my Higher Power to see things differently. It always works. It has never failed. I have told my family and friends this story, and they have asked for help, too. It works for them. Just take a moment, and in the quiet of your personal devotions, ask with your whole being. "Please let me see this (person or event) in a different way." Things will change and peace and love will change your life. You might find it difficult to stay in the fog when your heart is full of love and peace. I know that I do.

Asking for a change in perception, following the tenets of the Serenity Prayer, and breathing slowly and consciously are the three ways I use to stay away from the fog of everyday confusion. I also find that the longer I practice these principles in my everyday life the easier my life becomes. Today, life is good.

GREG FOX

TELEVISION NEWS ANCHOR / REPORTER
WESH-TV

The KISS Principle

Keep It Simple Stupid! Yes, the K.I.S.S. principle has been my guiding beacon in times when I find myself lost in deep, winding, emotionally stressful tunnels. Simplicity, for me, breeds clear thought, wise direction, and ease of decision making. Pinpoint a goal (or assess a problem) seek a solution, EXECUTE!

In this way, you eliminate distractions, prevent problems from magnifying, and keep a leash on runaway mental fatigue. For example, I'm a television news Reporter / Anchorman (by the way, I've always thought that name ANCHOR indicated I should have a large, heavy, ship's chain wrapped around my neck!) Anyway, as a TV newsman, I often have several story deadlines daily . . . Noon, 5pm, 5:30pm, 6pm, 11pm . . . not to mention breaking news cut-ins that interrupt regular programming. The sheer volume of work can be overwhelming.

Add to that, machines and news trucks that constantly break down, dozens of daily phone calls, communications (debates?). With producers, supervisors, photographers, editors, etc. . . . and that's ONE THICK FORMULA FOR MENTAL COLLAPSE! That doesn't even take into account the demands by various professional organizations and my church on my after-hours time. Suddenly, I can find myself sliding deep into emotional quicksand.

IT DOESN'T HAVE TO BE THAT WAY! Simplicity is my lifeline. Prioritize. Routinely, I line up my obligations in order of importance, and tackle them one at a time to the best of my ability. They are goals, each and everyone . . . a separate and satisfying achievement. By making daily tasks, "GOALS" (ones I know I can handle) I put my day in a logical order, and avoid the pressures fueled by disorganization.

Dealing with family is no different. Getting lunches and kids ready for school, car pool arrangements with other parents, play time, dinner time, bed time, birthday party plans, trips to visit relatives and friends on holidays . . . all represent sides in an endless tug-o-war. As a "REFEREE" along with my wife, we know we have to accept. . . not resent time sacrifices to cope.

It all goes back to simplicity: establish priorities, get down to business, be consistent. When I feel organized, I am more at ease, confident, and able-bodied to address the next challenge. Remember: Keep It Simple Stupid!

SCOTT HANSON

INVESTIGATIVE REPORTER
WESH-TV

I'm a firm believer in the "getting away from it all" school of fog clearing. Luckily, I know exactly where to go to do that. I gotta have a mountain.

The whole back to nature experience strips away all the distractions, and lays bare what has really gotten out of whack with my life, whatever it may be--too much work, too much pressure, too much time alone, too much time with crowds. Too much of any one thing seems to make the whole contraption of living tip.

Sometimes, the toughest part is noticing there's a problem. For me, my sense of humor is the first thing to go. It's good to have little things like that to watch for--little fog horns, you might say. When that happens, if you were to ask me what was wrong, I'd probably say work, or blame it on some little irritation I had that day. All of which would be wrong. That's the thing about the fog. You have to get away from it to see how big it is, and where it originates.

And so off to a mountain I go. There, where tiny streams cut deep gorges, and vast forests rejuvenate our atmosphere, I'm reminded exactly how much can go on without me. It's humbling. Suddenly, I'm in control of those pressures around me. I'm reminded nothing is created important--importance is something we endow upon things. Priorities snap back into place. There, on that mountain, I look into the valley. That's where fog tends to settle, after all. And I'm able to return to the lowlands carrying clarity inside me.

ED HEILAND

TELEVISION NEWS REPORTER
WESH-TV

What amazes me the most about day to day life is how quickly things can change. Like the weather, a bright sunny disposition can quickly change when life pressures are allowed to take over. At these times, tears and rain are synonymous. . . but unlike the weather, there are ways I have found to lift the mind-fog. For me, it's easiest to concentrate on what is important through my version of a communion with nature. . . yard work. Sure, part of that phrase is "work," but expending energy doing something you enjoy isn't labor. . . it's therapy.

I can trace the roots of what I experience now back to my Boy Scout days. In troop 371 there was always plenty to do. . . chopping wood, tying square knots to hold the towers and bridges you were building together, and cooking up meals based on the food you could find. They call it "survival camp" these days, but even then I always felt it was more of a "purification process." Just the act of getting away from civilization made you feel more self-reliant and able to cope. Those two night retreats made you forget about what we thought were pressures back then, schoolwork!

These days with family and home to

care for, a self-reliant retreat would actually be self-indulgent. So, the trick for me is to combine the needed yard maintenance, with my need for mental maintenance. It's amazing how your troubles can disappear along with the weeds. Trimming the hedges seems to "cutback" the number of problems. Call it a form of "aroma-therapy" but there's also a certain "smell" associated with working among the trees, grass, and flowers. That scent adds another dimension to the experience, and in it's own way, helps to heighten the experience. Often, just that slow walk behind the lawnmower, concentrating on making those straight-line cuts, can help me straighten out the problems that dog my life.

That's not to say the troubles aren't still there. Schoolwork didn't go away when I was a Boy Scout, and I've found life's woes remain even after cutting the grass. But instead of trying so hard to focus on what's wrong, I'm able to see problems or concerns in a different light.

Juxtaposing something complex, like life, with something so simple, like pulling weeds or cutting grass, seems to make things a bit more clear on those "mind-foggy" days.

DONALD LaRENE

HIGH SCHOOL TEACHER / COACH

When thunder showers are falling instead of soft dew, what do I do? First and foremost I thank God I'm still alive!

Are problems, decisions, deadlines, quotas, tests, and pleas of time and help making your day seem fuller than you may want, need, or think you can handle? Do the anxieties of a stress attack begin before the second phrase of the same song on your morning alarm? Are you weary and laden as you stagger out of bed to greet another threatening day? Gee, if life's not grand, then begin to take a stand, today! It's your life so take control. It can only be as grand as your master plan, so let's get started. One note however, though the magic wand and the bewitching twitch of the nose are preferred reminders in our instant society, reality overwhelmingly prevails, so be patient and count immediate gratification with small baby steps of success, improvement, progress, and control.

To know thyself and to thyself be true is a life long but worthy and needed endeavor and one that we have to develop day by day. Nothing can truly be done or a change made until you first realize or admit that, "Hey, I've

113

got a problem." It's like coming down with a cold. The sooner you realize the symptoms the sooner you can begin a remedy and the less severe the cold if you get it at all. And once you realize you have a problem then you can and must identify it. Next answer these questions making a list:

> *Which problems can I do something about now?
> *Which can wait awhile?
> *Which cannot be changed?

This list will depend upon or demand an order of priorities. That's why you need to make it and not someone else! Now take action. But there are multiples of problems you say. Stay with one. That's how this whole over populated and demanding world began. Begin by taking action. If you can't finish one entirely, go to the next one in order. Tomorrow put it back on your new list and place it accordingly. Each day, according to your priorities, make your list. Once you get your list to a manageable size, I try to keep it no more than ten, you're in control according to your terms. You set the limits. Remember, cleaning a mess or disorder is always more work and effort than maintaining order. Don't feel bad or foolish for being in this predicament. Life and living is a process. Know yourself, know your limits. I have two daughters, one spends all her free time cleaning her bedroom and it's never clean. The other rarely cleans and her room is always clean. It's the process, not the effort! Living is nothing more than solving problems, ie (making decisions and acting on them). Be like a bunny. First get off to a quick start--get started take action, and then if it's not resolved the first time, keep going, and going, and going (like the famous bunny) until it's resolved! What's your priority?

It's your life! Take control, and enjoy it, and you may find a soft gentle dew sweetening a rose along your path and you too may want to thank God you're still alive!

CLAIRE METZ

TELEVISION NEWS ANCHOR / REPORTER
WESH-TV

I run from one place to another all day, everyday. I feel like I'm always rushing to get somewhere. . . then rushing from there, on to my next destination. . .

I've actually stopped short and asked myself, "What are you doing. . . stop, give yourself a break." But there's no time. Between work and family, most of us find ourselves in the same spot. . . but I've only just realized I need a way to shake some of the tension off. . . a way to relax so that I can be a better wife, a better mother to my four children, a better employee at work.

And wonder of wonders, I've finally found something I love to do. When the 80's unleashed a generation of folks trying to get into shape, I wasn't one of them. I didn't have the patience. . . the time, the inclination. . .but before the body starts to go South, I've come to realize I better do something. . . This year, I started fast walking and with it, lost some weight. . . more importantly, I gained a new perspective. . .

I began, kind of half-heartedly. I clipped along, but it was a chore. I couldn't wait to go, so that I could be finished.

116

Something strange happened though, as the weeks passed. I found myself actually looking forward to the four mile, forty-five minute exercise. . . I wear head-sets. . . listen to music. . . but at the same time, I have a chance to think about the day. . . What's behind, what's ahead. I get a great physical workout four times a week. . . more importantly, it seems to lift my spirits. I'm re-energized. . . ready to talk with my husband. . . play with the kids. . . make the lunches, get dinner going. . . go over homework. . . The same routine the 90's woman follows. . . But with that spirited walk-run that has lifted my spirits. The exercise is actually addicting.

I have to do it now. . . I have to make time for myself. . . because when I do, I always have the best time with the ones I love. . .

MARC MIDDLETON

SPORTS ANCHOR
WESH TV

I'm a TV - guy. I've done the sports on the evening news for the past decade. We like to say, "It's not brain-surgery," and although no one lives or dies (hopefully) based upon what I do or say, the pressure can be intense. It's not only intense, it's unrelenting. Mine is a deadline business. There's dozens of deadlines each day. Everyday. I've learned to embrace deadlines, not only at work but in my personal life.

Sometimes the fog that clogs our lives and confuses us won't go away. Usually it gets worse. At best it leaves very slowly. The only sure way I've found out of the fog is to walk out. One step at a time. One foot in front of the other. The key is simply to begin. To take action. As soon as you move, the fog begins to dissipate. The closer you are to a goal, the more clearly you can see it. The really neat part is that when you're in a fog, even a step backwards is a step forward. Your vision begins to clear. A wrong move or two always begets a right move or two.

That's where the deadlines come in. Deadlines help you take that first step out of the fog. They help you (force you) to take the second and then the third step. Success is about momentum and deadlines get you moving. Moving off that spot where the fog is greatest. I've often wished there was a secret technique for lifting the fog, for making things happen the way I want them to. The truth is things don't happen. You make them happen. You set a deadline and take the first step. You take action. The more you use your "take action" muscle, the stronger it becomes.

Nike's slogan has become mine. "Just Do It," in truth, we're all working on a deadline. The really big deadline. The one that ends our lives. Don't get lost in the fog, unable to achieve what you want. Even if you're not sure where you're going, get going. Give yourself a deadline. Lots of deadlines. Deadlines everyday. Take the first step. Then the second. The third will become more obvious. The forth is a cinch. Soon the fog is lifted. Just Do It. And while you're at it, do it now. . .

GREG MORRIS

RADIO BROADCASTER

To relieve the day to day "brain strain" I enjoy a visit to my backyard sanctuary to watch and listen to the songbirds and squirrels. My water garden is also a great place to reflect and unwind.

At least once a month I trek out to one of several area wildlife refuges or state parks to let Mother Nature wash away the stress of city life. This also includes a canoe trip down the Wekiva River or a slow boat ride into the remote backwaters of the St. Johns River.

But to really blow out "brain strain" there's nothing quite like an extended trip into a remote Arizona or Utah canyon.

Carrying food, water and shelter across miles of wilderness brings out the best in my spirit. I'm able to put my life in perspective as I walk along trails and over huge cliff / boulder formations. The same trails once traveled by the "ancient ones," the Anasazi Indians.

Remnants of their existence in this harsh landscape includes pieces of pottery, corn cobs, cliff dwelling adobes, and stones used for weapons and tools.

That brings it all home. The fact that we mortal humans are only here for a short time and that too shall pass. Enjoy.

CHRIS MILIOTES

RESTAURANT MANAGER

Making Decisions in Our Lives

Whether I am approaching an opportunity or a problem in my life, the key to making the most of the opportunity or to solving the problem is focus. Tunnel-vision and wholehearted concentration on every detail are the route to a good decision. I weigh the pros and cons by listing anything that could go wrong. Just as important is determining how I should deal with the negatives and finally, whether they outweigh the positives. Although this may sound simplistic, it is not. The process requires "homework," attention to detail, and yes, eliminating wishful thinking by being very honest with myself.

My family has also found that it is always helpful to pray for guidance. We all have been blessed by the Lord's generosity, but are often tried and tested in our faith. His wisdom and His love will make itself known to you if you do keep the faith.

I feel that simplicity of the principles I have outlined can be comprehended and applied by everyone to make our way through life a little smoother.

TERRY SATER

TELEVISION NEWS ANCHOR
WESH-TV

I'm a husband, a father, and a television news anchor. The latter is a job where high pressure situations often sneak up on you from out of no where. But it's usually at the end of the day, after I leave the newsroom, that the evidence appears.

When the problems, stresses, and strains of life are about to overwhelm me. . . I usually pray. Going to God in prayer is an acceptance that there are many things in life that are beyond my control. . . so why not go to the person who is in control. Sometimes God's answers to my prayers aren't what I expect, but He knows best.

Success in life isn't about getting what you want. It's about how you respond no matter your circumstances. The Bible is full of those examples.

The sweetest things in life are usually gained after a lot of trial and error, struggle and strife. Remember. . . things that come easily are not appreciated as much as things that come with difficulty. Think about your own life experiences.

I also run or lift weights to help deal with being lost in the fog of life's challenges. You can also pray while you run. . . so you get double benefit. Add the endorphins gained from strenuous exercise into the mix and the stress can melt away. . . along with the pounds.

Sometimes I fail to deal with the fog as well as I would like. But it's more important to focus on doing better next time, than to focus on failure. I am by nature a perfectionist. That's a difficult thing to be, when I am far from perfect and live in an imperfect world.

I am married with three children very close in age. Daily life presents many challenges. I am an example for my children. How I respond to life's problems will set the stage for how they deal with them. That has added a new dimension, a new responsibility, and importance to being calm when facing turmoil. Who would you rather have lead you, someone who responds to a challenge with rage or someone who responds thoughtfully and calmly?

Here's a simple example. The other night, we had planned to barbecue steaks. We just moved to our current home and I hadn't used the grill since it had been handled by the movers. I turned to the propane and ignited the flame. My two oldest daughters, one almost two and the other going on four, were outside with their daddy watching the dinner preparations. We turned from the grill to do something else and suddenly we heard a pop.

The glass on the grill cover had shattered and was spread over the cooking grates as well as all over the ground. My three year old is very sensitive and immediately started to cry, but she also looked at me for my reaction. In a calm voice, I told her everything was okay as long as we were all okay. I told her we could cook the steaks inside and daddy could fix the grill another day. Her tears quickly stopped and a smile took their place. Her reaction was directly linked to my reaction. Because I didn't get upset, she quickly returned to being calm. This is a small event. But it is in the small things that we must start to make improvement, to find our way out of the fog. Eventually, if you work at it hard enough, you can also stay calm in the big events of life. It won't happen overnight. It takes a lot of hard work and remember. . . there is no substitute for hard work.

That's why I run. That's why I pray. Running is hard work. Surrendering in prayer can also be difficult. But if you do both long enough, you'll run right out of the fog.

JEANNETTE YUE

NEWS PHOTOGRAPHER
WESH-TV

Today is my last day on earth! As incorrect as I hope that thought is, I use it often to give myself perspective and new appreciation of my world and the people in it.

I lead a fast paced life. My days are filled with deadlines, short tempers, high expectations, and pressure. It is easy to get caught up in this whirlwind and lose sight of the "big picture." When I feel myself start to become overwhelmed I have learned a couple of tricks that smooth out the rough edges of my tension.

The first thing I try to do is find a place and about ten minutes of time to take a mini-mental vacation. In that period I mull over thoughts like the one I mentioned earlier and I remind myself that I am not running the show, God is. The last thing I do before returning to my day is to breathe a prayer. Almost instantly peace returns and I am refreshed. I can now look around me and I see that many of the pressures that were challenging me earlier are either of no consequence or are providing me a terrific opportunity to learn something new about myself and the world I live in.

These mini-vacations provide me a

chance to gain a fresh perspective and sometimes humility. Often I discover that the problem is really me. That's good news! I can work on myself but there is no way I can change anything or anybody else.

SING YUE

CLINICAL DIRECTOR - BRIDGES OF AMERICA

Picking Berries

When asked about my success, I only can say that I have been indebted to my cultural heritage and the faith that I followed. My conviction is that faith is always embedded in a life context which involves six basic virtues. Namely: Wisdom, Kindness, Righteousness, Integrity, Courage, and Perseverance. It is to be understood in terms of human relations based on spiritual personality. (A body-mind-spirit dimension).

My identity rests in the belief that God lives within me. Therefore, I constantly have to keep the balance between when to give up control in life and to trust in my own self-worthiness. As of now, I am still listening and voicing this spiritual conditioning in my summery journey of life. . . picking berries in the wild when wolves are roaming in the distance.

THE MULBERRY TREE

When I was a kid, I had a ritual of visiting an old mulberry tree that was, according to the size of its trunk, far older than its normal life span of 25 or 30 years. It was abundant with life and had long furrowed branches that were the home to plenty of birds and other wildlife. It grew at the top of a hill. At the bottom of the hill was a low section of ground where thousands of elephant ear plants grew. They were healthy, robust, thick and prolific. I would just sit there in total silence with my arms wrapped around my knees and just admire the whole scene. There was a lot going on in my silence.

In fact, I gained energy from the whole microcosm. I noticed the deeply furrowed trunk, the octopus-like branches, and the sparkling purple fruit that sang out to me like a beautiful song. I even noticed and appreciated the dead crunchy leaves that fell beneath the tree, contributing to its survival as they decayed and became mulch. The slope of the land with the unkept grass that tapered to the bottom of the hill where the elephant ears grew was a special place to me. The various sounds of the leaves touching each other as the wind swept through was beautiful to me. The birds fluttering in the trees was the most beautiful sound, almost like children laughing. The mulberry tree grew at the edge of a golf driving range. It was surrounded by native woods on three sides and was obviously the sentinel of the woods. One day while sitting in silence I heard a breaking, slicing noise through the foliage. It ended with a thump then silence again. I went to examine. I looked at the raised furrowed roots under the underbrush and saw a contented little wood duck, sitting calmly on a perfect little nest with a few golf balls around the edges of the nest. I slowly stepped back in silence, smiling and realizing that the mulberry tree was appreciated by far more than just me. By the way, I also loved the fact the mulberry tree had such a great sense of humor collecting all those golf balls in a furrowed root in a perfect little nest!

THE MULBERRY TREE

I know a place
Where the sun sparkles with a golden glow,
A light so bright
That the rays shimmer and glow,
A place where the mulberry grows.

High on a hill
Standing with arms outstretched,
Its armored coat ribbed and furrowed.
"Look at me here,
For all the world to see,"

Abundant with life,
Leaves come and go.
Life revolves in and around the scalloped branches
evolving seasonally from one beauty to another.
Not one more beautiful than the next.

I know a place that sparkles with light,
Radiant light, love and inspiration,
A place where the mulberry grows.